THE PALESTINE PROBLEM TODAY

The Author

Carl Hermann Voss, who received degrees from the University of Pittsburgh and from Union Theological Seminary in New York City, has held pastorates in Raleigh, Pittsburgh, and Brooklyn. A former executive of the Church Peace Union and of the World Alliance for International Friendship Through Religion, he is now chairman of the executive council of the American Christian Palestine Committee and a member of the faculty of the New School for Social Research. He has made several visits to Israel and the Arab countries.

The
Palestine Problem Today

ISRAEL AND ITS NEIGHBORS

by

Carl Hermann Voss

THE BEACON PRESS   BOSTON

Library of Congress catalog card number: 53-12778

Printed in U.S.A.

To all men and women of goodwill who have restored the ancient fertility of Palestine, Land of Israel, and have awakened in the Holy Land a renewed creativity of mind and spirit which impels "old men to dream dreams and young men to see visions."

Contents

Illustrations

Preface

As a Christian, I have for many years taken an interest in the development of Israel, the Jewish national homeland. At the same time I have felt concern for the fate of the Jewish people, whether in the free world or in totalitarian lands. I have been disturbed at the misinformation disseminated by those who do not sympathize with the aspirations of the state of Israel. It is this interest and this concern which have impelled me to prepare a new edition — the fifth — of my booklet originally called *Answers on the Palestine Question*.

In its earlier editions, *Answers on the Palestine Question* — an introductory statement giving background material on a complex subject — enjoyed a gratifyingly wide distribution during recent years. It evolved from an article written in the summer of 1946 at the request of *The Woman's Press*, national publication of the Young Women's Christian Association. Subsequent extensions and revisions of the material followed my visits to the Middle East and my continued study of the swiftly moving events in that sensitive area of the world.

Having now returned from my fourth visit to the eastern Mediterranean, I am once more endeavoring to state the basic issues of the Palestine problem as I see them today. On this journey to the land sacred to three major faiths of mankind — Islam, Judaism, and Christianity — I saw, as on my earlier trips, not only the Arab countries but also both parts of modern partitioned Palestine. One is the new state of Israel; the other is Arab Palestine, annexed on April 25, 1950, by the late King Abdullah to form an expanded Hashemite Kingdom of Jordan.

In the years between my first and this most recent visit, tremendous changes have taken place in Palestine. In 1947 Palestine was not, it must be confessed, a very holy land. Still administered by the British under the League of Nations Mandate, the country was dominated by tension and resentment, by violence and terrorism. The Mandate had urged the British to "facilitate Jewish immigration under suitable conditions and . . . encourage . . . close settlement by Jews . . . and intensive cultivation of the land" (Articles 6 and 11). But this the British had not done for some time.

There were conflicting claims by Arabs and Jews. The Arabs contended that the British had fulfilled their pledge in full measure. The Jews charged the British with a breach of faith. They cited the White Paper of 1939, which drastically limited Jewish immigration and thus nullified the League of Nations' objective — the establishment in Palestine of "a national home for the Jewish people." The slaughter of European Jewry and the need of stateless Jews for refuge in Palestine made even more urgent a solution for this difficult problem.

When I returned to the United States in late 1947, many people asked what I had found. I told my friends how impressed I had been by the courage and enterprise of the Jewish pioneers, how depressed by the continuing feudalism in the Arab lands, and how disturbed by the reluctance of the British to encourage land reclamation or to relieve the repressive police-state measures ordered by the then Foreign Secretary, Ernest Bevin. On one point at least, I was able to report, both Jews and Arabs were in accord: "The British must leave."

By the following May, the British had left. The United Nations Special Committee on Palestine (UNSCOP) had recommended to the U.N. the partition of Palestine as a means of reconciling Arab and Jewish claims. This was a compromise proposal that received the world tribunal's approval. The Palestinian Jews, in accordance with the U.N. partition resolution, proclaimed the state of Israel on May 14, 1948.

The Palestine problem was and is a conflict of rights as well as a complex of wrongs. The establishment of Israel was and is a creative answer to the world problem of anti-Semitism — an answer which might not be absolutely just to Arab rights in Palestine, but which seemed just in view of the granting of sovereignty to so many Arab states throughout the Middle East.

In the summer of 1949, I returned to the Middle East for an extensive survey of the new state of Israel. I was unable to secure an entry permit from the Jordan government to cross from Israel into the Old City of Jerusalem; for the truce in the Arab-Israel war of 1948 had not — as even today — been transmuted into a peace treaty, despite herculean efforts by Dr. Ralph J. Bunche, Acting U.N. Mediator.

Israel, then only one year old, was youthful and ebullient. Throbbing with activity and fired by high ideals, it was the most dynamic land I had seen, whether in North America or Europe, Asia or Africa. I could well understand why Count Folke Bernadotte, U.N. Mediator for Palestine, shortly before his tragic death in the autumn of 1948, had described Israel as "a vibrant reality."

I recalled the words of the late Dr. Norman MacLean, onetime chaplain to King George VI and former moderator of the General Assembly in Scotland, who in 1941 had said:

> There is no experiment in human uplift now to be seen on the face
> of the earth which can compare to the work of the Jews in Palestine.
> If I were a Jew, I would deem it the highest honor life can hold to take
> part in a work so noble.

This "experiment in human uplift" took on new significance for me later when, on my way to Israel, I stood before the Arch of Titus in Rome. I reflected on the strange fate of the Jewish people, illustrated so graphically on the frieze which depicts the destruction of the Second Temple in 70 A.D.

It was Nero, last of the Caesars, who had sent Vespasian and his son Titus from Rome to the Levant, with orders to subjugate the Jews, destroy Jerusalem, and conquer Judea. When Vespasian returned to be crowned Emperor, Titus remained and laid awful siege to Jerusalem. After two terror-filled years of starvation and pestilence, the city fell, as the historian reminds us, "amid circumstances of unparalleled horror."

Titus returned to Rome in pomp. A great procession brought him, his loot and booty, prisoners and hostages, to the triumphal arch which was to bear his name. Here were carved the Jewish Menorah, the seven-branched candelabrum, and, as a boast for all posterity to read, the terse phrase "Judea capta."

"Judea capta" signified more than Judea's capture. It meant that Jerusalem, City of Peace, had been razed; that Judaism, the belief in One God and rival faith to emperor worship, had been expunged; and that the Jewish people had been dispersed. Titus wanted the children of Israel, "despised and rejected of men," to know in the year of the destruction of their Temple that, from that time on and evermore, they would have no homeland — only prayers and tears.

But Titus was wrong.

Today, as the traveler comes by ship across the blue of the Mediterranean toward Judea reborn, he discerns in the distance a thin strand of sand which has been pushed toward the sea by the ever-growing green of farm settlements and the teeming cities of the new Israel. He knows then how ephemeral was Titus' boast, how miracle-working the tenacity, the faith, and the will to live of a "stiff-necked people."

If the modern tourist comes by plane, he will have perhaps an even more stirring experience. He may circle over the cities of Haifa and Tel Aviv before landing, even as the Psalmist had sung centuries ago, "on the wings of the morning" at the modern airport at Lydda.

An Israeli boards the plane and greets the traveler with the age-old salutation "Shalom! Shalom u'vracha! Peace and all blessings unto thee and thine!" He is native-born, a sabra — that is, "fruit of the cactus," rough and tough in outer mien, but soft and tender within. He stamps the passport with a seal bearing the same design of the seven-branched candelabrum to be found on the Arch of Titus; but on either side of the Menorah are palm branches, symbols of peace. Beneath it is not the phrase "Judea capta," but rather the word which neither hate nor persecution of nineteen centuries has erased, the name Titus thought he had destroyed forever — *Israel*.

No visitor to Israel and the Arab lands can escape the impact of such historic associations, for he finds ancient and modern juxtaposed. I felt as though the twentieth century had suddenly come to these starved, parched, eroded lands, which once were the cradle of civilization and which now, in our day, experience the creativity of the Zionist idea.

A modern pilgrim to Palestine, standing on the dock of the harbor of Haifa, Israel's major port, may delight in the beauty of the bay, so like the exquisite Gulf of Naples in its symmetry and loveliness of sea and sky. Standing there, he may see a real homecoming, as into Haifa's waters steam the ships bearing Jews who come literally from the four corners of the earth: Talmudists from Lithuania, Latvia, and Poland; unlettered but devout Jews from Turkestan and Afghanistan; café artists from London and Paris; sophisticates from Vienna and Rome; black-skinned Jews from Ethiopia; stalwart pioneers from Australia, Canada, the United States, New Zealand, Scandinavia and South Africa. They come, a colorful procession of humanity, imbued with a fervor of faith and longing that has sustained them in distant lands over seas and continents. Even the irreligious cannot forget the ancient promise: "The Lord made a covenant with Abraham, saying, 'Unto thee and thy seed have I given this land.'"

They hear again the prescient words of Jeremiah: "The Lord shall set His hand again the second time to recover the remnants of His people, and He shall assemble the outcast of Israel and gather together the depressed of Judah from the four corners of the earth."

Because I had seen the persecuted and dispossessed in the detention centers of Germany and Austria, it was a memorable experience now to see these same men and women come home at last. They were coming home from lands of death and dispersal to a land of life and light.

It was a fulfillment of the prophecy of Isaiah: "The people that walked in darkness have seen a great light; they that dwelt in the land of the shadow of death, upon them hath the light shone." So was it, too, for Jews who had left the caverns and cellars of North Africa or the bleak wastes of feudal Yemen.

In a *ma'abara*, a work village on the slopes of Mount Carmel not far from Elijah's cave, I talked to a bizarre type of Jew — a Jew from Bagdad, purportedly descended from those who did not return with Ezra and Nehemiah from the Babylonian exile to rebuild the Temple 2,500 years ago. In garb that made him almost indistinguishable from his Arab cousin, and speaking the Arabic tongue, he seemed incongruous in this modern setting of the new Israel; yet this Iraqi Jew gave new meaning to a sentence I had learned in my youth: "Behold I shall bring them from the north country and I shall gather them from the coasts of the earth. A great company shall return thither."

As I walked through the crowded, noisy streets of Tel Aviv or along the broad avenues of beautiful, majestic Jerusalem, rode up to picturesque Galilee or down to the newly populated desert areas of the Negev, ancient words haunted me: "He shall cause them that come of Jacob to take root: Israel shall blossom and bud, and shall fill the face of the world with fruit. . . . Thou shalt be a blessing . . . and in thee shall all families of the earth be blessed. . . . The wilderness and the solitary places shall be glad for thee. The desert shall rejoice, and shall blossom like the rose."

In both Israel and the Arab lands on these visits, I asked questions — many of them similar to questions I have been asked by lecture audiences throughout the United States. The answers, as factual as I can make them, are to be found in these pages. The facts and figures, dates and data do not, however, express the deep emotion I experienced in revisiting these ancient-modern sites. They do reflect my gratitude for the warm-hearted hospitality of the Israelis and the traditional courtesy and gracious welcome of the Arabs. They highlight my concern for the well-being and progress of the Arab states, my hope of permanence for both Israel and the Arab nations, and my prayer that the day shall soon be at hand when Israelis and Arabs join hands to beat their swords into plowshares, when they shall learn war no more and taste the fruits of peace.

However, recent disturbances and forays across the borders between Israel and the neighboring Arab states, particularly the Hashemite Kingdom of the Jordan, have been brought to the attention of the U.N. Security Council. These events highlight the importance of the Palestine problem. I hope that the issues discussed and the facts presented in this book will be of value in understanding Israel in the Middle East complex.

CARL HERMANN VOSS

New York City
Autumn 1953

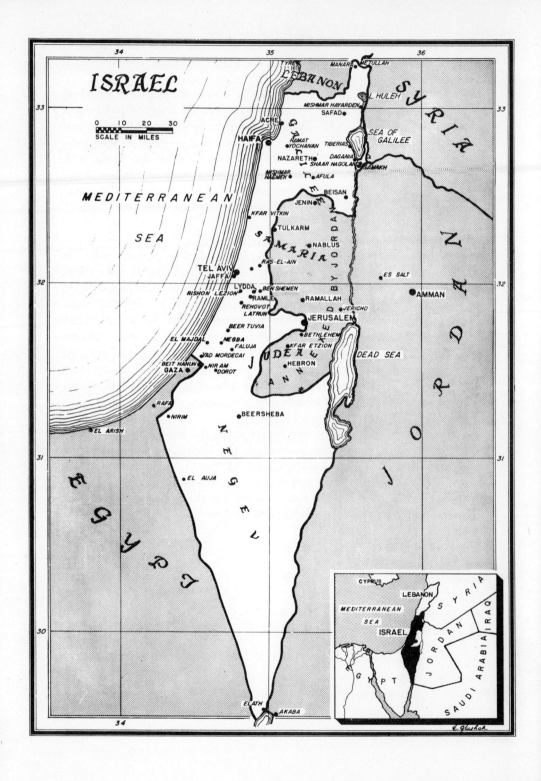

CHAPTER ONE

Unto Thee and Thy Seed

Why is the problem of Palestine so important?

In the religious history of mankind, Palestine — the land of Israel — has been cherished not only by Moslems and Christians but also by the Jewish people, for whom the Holy Land holds special meanings of history, revelation, and inspiration. The spiritual heritage of Islam, Christendom, and Judaism explains, however, only a part of the world's interest in an Eastern land smaller than the state of Massachusetts.

The ancient Mediterranean area, which reflects the waning power of two great empires, British and French, is coveted by dictators and their cabals in Cairo, Damascus, and Bagdad. Today it is an important area for both the United States and the USSR. Our own country, aware of the strategic value of American oil concessions there and concerned with the welfare of all the peoples in that region and the safeguarding of democratic ideals, grants military support and technical assistance. Soviet Russia, casting its eyes on the Middle East's oil resources, hopes to exploit for its own purposes the social, economic, and political unrest of feudal lands.

The Palestine problem is of importance, too, because it symbolizes human despair and human achievement. The story involves both the League of Nations, which, a generation ago, entrusted Great Britain with the Mandate over Palestine, and the United Nations, which, in 1947-48, exercised the wisdom of a Solomon to solve the Arab-Jewish-British impasse. Every civilized person should be concerned with the Jewish and Arab refugee problems, with the plight of a million and a half homeless men, women, and children of a common Semitic origin. And the issue is instinct with the will to survive, to consummate a 1,900-year-old dream — the dream of those who have taken an ancient land and made it fruitful, who have established, with the blessing of the United Nations, a new state, a free democracy, the republic of Israel.

What is unique about the rise of the republic of Israel?

For a nation to reappear after an interval of years, even decades, would in any event be unusual; but the emergence of Israel as a state after an interlude of almost two millennia is remarkable. National independence has almost invariably been achieved where a nationality group has continued to live uninterruptedly in its traditional territory. Israel is a notable exception, for the Jewish people, dispersed from their own soil, endured centuries of cruel persecution and wandered from one land to another for more than nineteen centuries.

Before re-creating their nationhood, the Jewish people were forced to take first steps. We all recall the dramatic story of the colonists who, in America and in most of the British dominions, ploughed the plains, scaled the mountains, forded the rivers, and built the cities. We remember, too, the intense struggle for freedom that forged Ireland.

Of such a dual process was Israel born, with this difference: Palestine's plains were deserts; its hills and valleys were wastelands and sand dunes; and its rivers were *wadis,* which in torrents carried the winter rains and priceless topsoil into the sea.

In another important aspect, the quest for a Jewish national homeland paralleled the historic pattern of the establishment of other nations: the Jews, like the American colonists, achieved their nation's independence by revolution and war. After the Palestinian Jews had rebelled against the White Paper policy of the British Mandatory, and after the United Nations had voted partition of the land, Britain ordered the withdrawal of its armed forces in May of 1948. The proclamation of the state of Israel followed forthwith. Since the Arab nations rejected the U.N. decision, and since the U.N. did not have the means to enforce its decision, the Israelis were left to defend themselves against the Arab armies sent by five member states of the Arab League to prevent partition and the establishment of the state of Israel.

If the Israelis had not repelled the invaders, the U.N. truce negotiations would hardly have been able to save even an enclave in the new state.

Israel's uniqueness lies, therefore, neither in colonization nor in its struggle for freedom, but rather in achieving the seemingly impossible task of restoring the children of Israel, scattered for almost two thousand years over the face of the earth, to their ancient homeland and building there the third Jewish commonwealth.

What was the Jewish connection with Palestine?

The age-old longing of the Jewish people for Palestine as a national home-land has echoed down through the centuries in the prayer, "Next year in Jerusalem!" Now that prayer is fulfilled; but it is still repeated as a witness to spiritual and cultural links in a historic chain of events that began with the migration of the Hebrews from Egypt in the fourteenth century before the Christian era, when Moses led his people to the Promised Land.

At the time of the Babylonian exile six centuries before the Christian era, and after the Dispersion which began in 69-70 A.D. with the sack of Jerusalem by the Romans, the Jews nurtured that hope; and, through the next eighteen centuries, a people dispersed throughout the world yearned cease-lessly for the Return and remained confident that it would take place.

Palestine has played a singular role in the history of the Jewish people for more than three thousand years. It was indisputably their land from the time of Joshua's conquest in 1300 B.C., through the periods of the First and Second Temples, and long after the Roman conquest of Jerusalem in 69-70 A.D. As late as the fourth century of the Christian era, the Jews still constituted the majority of the population of Palestine. Despite invasions and changes of rule, large numbers remained in the country until the First Crusade in 1090 A.D., when they were almost wiped out. In the years between that period and the beginnings of modern Jewish resettlement in the nineteenth century, they continued to come to Palestine in groups of hundreds and of thousands in spite of many difficulties.

The link between the People Israel and the Promised Land of Israel may have been invisible to all but visionaries, "God-intoxicated men," and the Jews themselves during the long centuries of dispersal; but it was as powerful as though forged in steel. Indeed, history has recorded few dreams held so valiantly for so long by so many as the dream that some day the Jews would re-establish nationhood on their ancient soil.

The Patriarch Abraham proclaimed this indissoluble connection: "The Lord made a covenant . . . saying, 'Unto thee and thy seed have I given this land.'" Ezra and Nehemiah, Yehuda Halevi, and — in modern times —Theodor Herzl, Chaim Weizmann, and David Ben-Gurion restated this pledge of several millennia. And, miraculously, it came to pass. The ancient promise, reiterated by prophecies and reflected in the prayers of the pious, was fulfilled. Not only Jews stood in awe but non-Jews as well — for the Zionist hope, in this fulfillment, had overtones of the Eternal.

3

How did Christians view these hopes for a Jewish national homeland?

Not only were Jews sustained by that dream, but many great Christians sought to aid what Professor Martin Buber has described as "the historical destiny of the people of Israel." The imaginations of theologians and statesmen, poets and philosophers were fired by the idea that the People of the Book would some day be restored to the Land of the Book.

While some Christian groups opposed this Zionist restoration, other Christians interpreted Jewish redemption as a prerequisite to the Second Coming of the Messiah, to be followed by the conversion of the Jews and the Millennium.

Others, less zealous and evangelical but certain that Old Testament prophecy would be fulfilled, considered the return of the Jews to Palestine as an important step for the advancement of mankind, and still others advocated the restoration of Israel as a refuge for the persecuted and as a partial answer to the evil of anti-Semitism.

The movement grew and with it the concept, so that a great spiritual movement evolved, not only in British circles, but also among Italians, Frenchmen, Russians, and Americans.

Many a heart was stirred by Lord Byron's lamentation in his "Hebrew Melodies":

> The wild dove hath her nest, the fox his cave,
> Mankind their country — Israel but the grave!

Napoleon, who had contemplated enlisting Jewish support for his Middle East campaigns by promising to restore Jerusalem, reflected the general acknowledgment in his time of the interest of the Jews in Palestine.

In similar fashion, the pleas of Colonel George Gawler, a former governor of South Australia, in 1845; of the Earl of Shaftesbury in 1840 and 1876; of Henry Dunant, founder of the Red Cross, in 1876; and of Laurence Oliphant, British M.P., in 1882, indicated how strong an appeal the concept of "Zion Restored" had for nineteenth-century Europe.

One of the most eloquent voices was that of George Eliot. In 1876, her book *Daniel Deronda* described the Israel to be established:

> The outraged Jew shall have a defense in the court of nations, as the outraged Englishman or American. And the world will gain as Israel gains. For there will be a community in the van of the East which carries the culture and sympathies of every great nation in its bosom; and there will be a land set for the halting place of enmities.

4

How recent is American Christian support for this movement?

Many Christians in America have been aware of Jewish sufferings through the ages. Even if vaguely, they have been sensitive to the lament of the sage who, more than five centuries ago, wrote:

> If all the seas were ink, and all the reeds pens, and all the peoples scribes, it would not be enough to record all the misfortunes of the Jews in a single year.

Such an awareness explains in part the approval given by John Adams and Thomas Jefferson to the Zionist plans of Mordecai Noah in the early part of the nineteenth century.

It was not unusual, therefore, when Christian concern was expressed in the petition presented on March 5, 1891, by the Rev. William E. Blackstone to President Benjamin Harrison and Secretary of State James G. Blaine. The petition requested these men to use their good offices and influence with the governments of Europe "to secure the holding, at an early date, of an international conference to consider the condition of the Israelites and their claims to Palestine as their ancient home."

Dr. Blackstone had visited Palestine and Syria in 1889. With a foresight borne out by events two generations later, he made a careful study that convinced him that "the land of Palestine is capable of remarkable development, both agriculturally and commercially."

Blackstone seems to have conveyed this enthusiasm to others, for his petition carried the signatures of four hundred newspaper publishers, editors, public officials, clergymen, leaders in business and finance, and members of the bar and judiciary. They included Chief Justice Melville W. Fuller; Cardinal Gibbons of Baltimore; Congressman (later President) William McKinley; Speaker of the House Thomas B. Reed; the mayors of Chicago, New York, Philadelphia, Baltimore, and Boston; the governor of Massachusetts; the Archbishop of Chicago; a number of Protestant Episcopal and Methodist bishops; and six members from the respective faculties of McCormick and Chicago Theological Seminaries.

Business leaders on the list included Cyrus H. McCormick, Philip D. Armour, Potter Palmer, J. Pierpont Morgan, Cyrus W. Field, John D. Rockefeller, Russell Sage, Charles Scribner, and J. Henry Harper.

A quarter-century later, during World War I, and a half-century later, in World War II, Christian support emerged once again to give powerful impetus to the movement which sought a haven of refuge and the guarantee of a homeland for the harassed Jewish people.

KIBBUTZ MERHAVIA IN THE VALLEY OF JEZREEL

WITH HILLS OF GALILEE IN THE BACKGROUND

How did the Zionist movement of modern times originate?

Zionism did not originate with Theodor Herzl at the First Zionist Congress of 1897 in Basle. He was one among many who helped to crystallize the longings of the Jewish people for Palestine as a homeland. In the nineteenth century he had many precursors. Foremost among them were three men:

(1) Moses Hess, who in 1862 wrote the controversial *Rome and Jerusalem: The Latest National Question.*

(2) Leo Pinsker, who wrote the provocative *Auto-Emancipation: An Admonition to His Brethren by a Russian Jew,* spurring "The Lovers of Zion" in Russia to found the first agricultural settlements in Palestine in that year, 1882.

(3) Rabbi Samuel Mohilver, who in 1882 went to Paris to interest Baron Edmond Rothschild in Jewish colonization in Palestine. As a result of his efforts, five Jewish colonies in Palestine were founded.

For Herzl himself, the catalyst was the Dreyfus case, where an obviously anti-Jewish prejudice prevailed in the judicial proceedings. Captain Alfred Dreyfus was unjustly convicted of espionage and sentenced to Devil's Island in 1894. Theodor Herzl, a Viennese playright and journalist, reported the trial. He poured his anger into a widely read book, *Der Judenstaat (The Jewish State).*

In it, he referred to the "Jewish question . . . a hangover of the Middle Ages, of which the modern civilized nations, with the best will in the world, cannot rid themselves" and demanded an end to the national homelessness of the Jewish people.

Herzl foretold such Israeli technological advances as the extraction of minerals from the Dead Sea and the development of hydroelectric projects in the Jordan Valley. He sought political guarantees for a Jewish state and urged widespread migration of Jews to Palestine.

But, like Moses of old, Herzl did not live to see the fulfillment of his vision. In 1904, at the age of forty-four, he died, distraught by dissension among his fellow Jews, worn by opposition from anti-Zionists, dejected by rebuffs from the Turkish Sultan and the German Kaiser.

Yet it was Herzl's spirit that gave life and meaning to the Zionist movement. In subsequent decades, such diverse yet gifted men as Max Nordau and Chaim Weizmann, Martin Buber and Judah Magnes, Louis Dembitz Brandeis and Louis Lipsky, Stephen S. Wise and Abba Hillel Silver have helped give body to that spirit.

Does Zionism imply "dual allegiance"?

In ancient days when many Jews lived outside the Jewish Commonwealth of Palestine, the rabbis were asked for a clear ruling on the subject of allegiance. Their answer, as recorded in the Talmud, was: "The law of the land in which you live is the law by which you shall abide."

Every country that has offered Jews the status of citizenship has evoked on their part the response of loyalty — in law-abiding behavior in peacetime and in readiness for supreme sacrifice in time of war. The history of the United States is ample demonstration of this.

The Zionist movement was created to meet the problem of Jews living in countries which did not give Jews the full rights of citizenship. The founders of this movement were convinced that Jews in Central and Eastern Europe — where nearly 80 per cent of all the Jews then lived — could never attain the status of full citizenship in those countries. That prognosis was amply and cruelly proved during the Hitler period. In the establishment of a Jewish state they saw the one way out, and they called on Jews in free countries to help them.

Now Israel is an independent state. To it American Jews owe no political allegiance. That they want to help Israel is understandable; that they are prepared to aid Jews to settle in Israel is laudable; that they take a special interest in the religious, cultural, and spiritual institutions developing there is a factor of significance in their own spiritual development.

There are many parallels to this in American history. One instance is that of the Irish who, in the United States, were the major source of strength of the movement which resulted in a free Eire. Such cultural pluralism has been one of the ways in which Americans of European background have helped promote the cause of freedom in the Old World.

The wisest words written to answer this accusation of dual allegiance were those of the late Louis D. Brandeis, Associate Justice of the U. S. Supreme Court. As a leader among American Zionists and American Jews, he said:

> Let no American imagine that Zionism is inconsistent with patriotism. Multiple loyalties are objectionable only if they are inconsistent. A man is a better citizen of the United States for being also a loyal citizen of his state, and of his city; for being loyal to his family, and to his profession or trade; for being loyal to his college or lodge. . . . Every American Jew who aids in advancing the Jewish settlement in Palestine, though he feels that neither he nor his descendants will ever live there, will likewise be a better man, a better American for doing so.

CHAPTER TWO

His Majesty's Government View With Favor

How did Britain become involved in Palestine?

On December 9, 1917, General Allenby led his Expeditionary Force to the walls of Jerusalem. His brilliant military campaign had routed the Turks from Palestine. Followed by his men, Allenby walked through the Jaffa Gate and took possession in the name of King George V.

Thus ended and thus began an era. To one of the world's most storied lands a new dispensation had come. The Ottoman Empire, ruler of Palestine almost without a break for four hundred years, was crumbling. Palestine became a prize sought by both French and British. To the French, it meant control of the Levant; to the British, it meant a solid power bloc stretching from Egypt to India. The Russians also had special claims, for many Palestinian Christians were members of the Russian Orthodox Church.

On November 2, 1917, the British War Cabinet put aside the secret 1916 Sykes-Picot Treaty (designed to share control of Palestine with the French) and issued a "declaration of sympathy with Jewish Zionist aspirations." This later came to be known as the Balfour Declaration, after Arthur James Balfour, then Secretary of State for Foreign Affairs:

> His Majesty's Government view with favor the establishment in Palestine of a national home for the Jewish people, and will use their best endeavors to facilitate the achievement of this object, it being clearly understood that nothing shall be done which may prejudice the civil and religious rights of existing non-Jewish communities in Palestine, or the rights and political status enjoyed by Jews in any other country.

In 1920, Great Britain was chosen by the League of Nations to administer the Mandate for Palestine, to put "into effect the Balfour Declaration," to "facilitate Jewish immigration," to "encourage close settlement by Jews on the land," and to "be responsible for placing the country under such political, administrative and economic conditions as will secure the establishment of the Jewish National Home."

Was the establishment of a Jewish state endorsed by the United States government?

The United States government, at the invitation of the British, helped to formulate the Balfour Declaration.

In January 1919, the intelligence section of the American delegation to the Paris Peace Conference presented a comprehensive memorandum for the settlement of Middle East problems, recommending that the Arabs have independence in Syria, Mesopotamia, and Arabia and that the Jews have independence in Palestine. The exact words were these:

> That the Jews be invited to return to Palestine and settle there, being assured by the Conference of all proper assistance in so doing that may be consistent with the protection of the personal (especially the religious) and the property rights of the non-Jewish population, and being further assured that it will be the policy of the League of Nations to recognize Palestine as a Jewish State as soon as it is a Jewish State in fact.

On March 2, 1919, President Woodrow Wilson reiterated his "personal approval of the Declaration" and added:

> I am, moreover, persuaded that the Allied nations, with the fullest concurrence of our Government and people, are agreed that in Palestine shall be laid the foundations of a Jewish Commonwealth.

Wilson's support did not waver, even after he received an anti-Zionist report — that of the King-Crane Commission, which he had appointed to study the problems of the region.

The desired ends remained therefore the same: *a democratic settlement by the victorious Allies to insure freedom and independence for the Arab lands and to lay the foundations for a Jewish state in Palestine.*

Each subsequent President — Harding, Coolidge, Hoover, Roosevelt, and Truman — put himself on record in favor of these objectives. The same was true of the Congress in 1922 and 1945, as well as of many State legislatures and the platforms of both major political parties. President Eisenhower has stated: "Our forces saved the remnant of the Jewish people of Europe for a new life and a new hope in the reborn land of Israel. Along with all men of good will, I salute the young state and wish it well."

In 1924, the United States government signed an Anglo-American convention to approve the Mandate as entrusted to Great Britain and to reserve the right to be consulted about proposed changes in the administration of Palestine.

Did the Arabs accept the Balfour Declaration?

The Arabs accepted the Balfour Declaration, in letter or in spirit, not once but on at least three occasions:

(1) In June 1918, Dr. Chaim Weizmann was welcomed in Amman by the Emir Feisal and by T. E. Lawrence. The three—representing respectively Zionists, Arabs, and British — agreed that the Middle East needed both Arab and Jew.

. (2) On January 3, 1919, an agreement was signed between the Emir Feisal, acting on behalf of the Arabs, and Dr. Weizmann, representing the World Zionist Organization. The two men, "mindful of the racial kinship and racial bonds existing between the Arabs and the Jewish people," agreed "that the surest means of working out the consummation of their national aspirations is through the closest possible collaboration in the development of the Arab state and Palestine." Article 3 of that agreement looked to the fulfillment of "the British Government's Declaration of November 2, 1917." Article 4 called for "all necessary measures . . . to encourage and stimulate immigration of Jews into Palestine on a large scale, and as quickly as possible to settle Jewish immigrants upon the land through closer settlement and intensive cultivation of the soil."

(3) Two months later, during the Paris Peace Conference, the Emir Feisal wrote a letter to Felix Frankfurter, now Associate Justice of the U. S. Supreme Court, and noted:

> The Arabs, especially the educated among us, look with deepest sympathy on the Zionist movement. . . . We will wish the Jews a hearty welcome home. . . . We are working together for a reformed and revived Near East, and our two movements complete one another. The Jewish Movement is national and not imperialist. Our Movement is national and not imperialist, and there is room in Syria for us both. Indeed, I think that neither can be a real success without the other.

Arab leaders later repudiated these expressions of friendship and co-operation, charging that, since the promises made to them by the Allies had been broken, they were released from any obligations under the treaty with Dr. Weizmann.

T. E. Lawrence, champion of Arab aspirations, thought otherwise. He said: "I must put on record my conviction that England is out of the Arab affair with clean hands."

Time has attested the truth of his statement. In our day each of the Arab states and the Jews in Palestine have attained independence and nationhood.

Was Palestine an Arab country?

Although Palestine has been a battleground for warring Arab nations and a coveted prize of several Arab empires, there has never been an independent Arab state of Palestine. While the Arabs, including Moslems and Christians, were a numerical majority, only the Jewish community showed the characteristics of a state or nation.

As a matter of historical record, the Jews never relinquished their claim to the land, a claim specifically acknowledged in the Preamble of the Mandate, which emphasized "the historical connection of the Jewish people with Palestine" and "the grounds for reconstituting their National Home in that country."

Throughout the centuries, Jews never ceased to foster immigration to their Promised Land and there was always a Jewish community in Palestine. Jews in all parts of the earth taxed themselves in its behalf. Hebrew literature throughout the centuries is replete with references to *Eretz Israel,* Land of Israel.

As early as the seventh century, a Jewish army from Palestine aided the Persians in their struggle against the rulers of Byzantium. So cruel were the forces of Christian Byzantium that the Jews welcomed the Arabs' conquest of Palestine in 634-638 A.D. and even joined forces with them.

Islamic empires ruled Palestine until 1071 A.D., and for the past nine centuries the land has known no rule by Arabs. Under the Ottoman Empire of the Turks, the policy of despoliation continued; the hillsides were denuded of trees and the valleys robbed of their topsoil.

The Arab population of Palestine was small and limited until Jewish resettlement restored the barren land and drew to it Arabs from neighboring countries. When organized Jewish colonization began in 1882, there were fewer than 150,000 Arabs in the land. The great majority of the Arab population in recent decades were comparative newcomers — either late immigrants or descendants of persons who had immigrated into Palestine in the previous seventy years.

One more fact is important. In the twelve and a half centuries between the Arab conquest in the seventh century and the beginnings of the Jewish return in the 1880's, Palestine was laid waste. Its ancient canal and irrigation systems were destroyed and the wondrous fertility of which the Bible spoke vanished into desert and desolation. The rehabilitation, now carried on with vigor and imagination by the modern Israelis, began in 1882 under the careful planning and courageous colonization of the Jews; and it found wider scope under the Mandatory of the British.

13

Was the British Mandate successful?

The British government administered the League of Nations Mandate with some success and considerable failure, a fact noted often by the Permanent Mandates Commission in Geneva.

Certainly the Jewish pioneering efforts were successful. They restored fertility to the soil and planted trees on bleak hillsides. They erected towns on wasteland, villages and farms amid ancient Biblical sites, and created the *Vaad Leumi* as an embryonic government — ultimately to develop into the governing body of the new Israel. The Arabs, too, enjoyed a much higher level of living than millions of their kinsfolk in neighboring lands. A comparatively high level of culture and economic well-being prevailed in Palestine, even in the Depression years of the 1930's. For this, some credit should go to the British Mandate.

But there was failure too. Neither Jew nor Arab was at ease with British officials, who seemed to be carrying the "white man's burden." Jew and Arab at one time or another each considered himself rejected and claimed that the other was the favorite of the Mandatory Power. This was not altogether fantasy, for the British were unwilling or perhaps unable to establish a policy firm enough to resolve inevitable differences between Jew and Arab. One commission of inquiry after another visited Palestine and made recommendations, most of which were not implemented by the British.

The simple, overwhelming fact was the existence in Palestine of a fully organized, actually independent, modern Jewish community lacking only political sovereignty. Such a group could never have been swallowed up in an Arab state as anticipated by Malcolm MacDonald's White Paper in 1939.

The British were somewhat less than successful in restraining the ex-Mufti of Jerusalem, Haj Amin el Husseini, from creating "disturbances" in the 1920's, 1930's, and 1940's — latterly as an agent of the Nazis during World War II. Later the ex-Mufti co-operated with the Cominform during the 1950's, as he had in 1929 with the Comintern.

The Mandate period was a constant vexation for the British. It was especially trying for Winston Churchill, who, more than three decades ago, foresaw the creation "in our own lifetime by the banks of the Jordan a Jewish State under the Protection of the British Crown." During World War II, he confessed that the presence of his old friend, Dr. Weizmann, disturbed him greatly, because Churchill could not answer Weizmann's requests to open the doors of Palestine for Jewish refugees from Europe who were trying to escape the holocaust of Hitlerism.

14

IMMIGRANT JEW FROM YEMEN DRIVING TRACTOR

CHAPTER THREE

The Swastika and the Star of David

What were the results of Hitler's persecution of the Jewish people?

In January 1933, President von Hindenburg of Germany, then all but senile, named Adolf Hitler chancellor of the Republic. This placed in power a man and a party crazed with the desire for revenge against the victors of World War I and imbued with an incredible racist concept which held the Jewish people responsible for the ills of the world.

Nazi anti-Semitism first victimized German and Austrian Jewry, later Jews in other European countries. Ultimately, Hitler's psychotic hatred spread until it affected Jewish communities everywhere.

Legends of usurers and blood-ritual murders circulated again. Forgeries such as the *Protocols of the Elders of Zion* were revived. German Jews were ousted from positions of cultural and economic eminence. Leaders of political organizations were tortured in concentration camps.

Of Germany's Jewish population of 650,000, some managed to escape. Those who remained in Germany cherished a vain hope that the Hitler regime might fall. In 1939, they too were doomed. With millions of Jews from Hitler-occupied lands, they were murdered during the early 1940's — beaten, asphyxiated, burned to death in the gas chambers and cremation furnaces of Bergen-Belsen, Treblinka, Auschwitz. In Poland, Rumania, and Hungary, the anti-Semitism of decades past flared anew.

By 1945, Hitler's Reich lay in ruins. Of Europe's eight and a half million Jews, more than six million had been annihilated in a mass murder so foul and shameful that even now the human mind can scarcely comprehend its full enormity. Many hundreds of thousands had fled to other continents; but at the end of the war at least a million European Jews were still alive in desperate straits. Of these, 230,000 were homeless refugees in the displaced-persons camps of Germany and Austria.

Why did not the United States absorb the Jewish refugees from Europe?

Except for a few thousands annually, Jewish D.P.'s from Europe did not come to the United States. The reasons were twofold: (1) our immigration laws imposed restrictions on newcomers, particularly those from Eastern and Central Europe; and (2) more than 90 per cent of the Jewish D.P.'s wanted to remake their lives in Palestine rather than America.

This latter fact was underscored by the report of Earl G. Harrison, United States representative on the Intergovernmental Committee on Refugees, sent by President Harry S. Truman to make a special inquiry about stateless and displaced Jews:

> With respect to possible places of resettlement for those who may be stateless or who do not wish to return to their homes, Palestine is definitely and preeminently the first choice. Many now have relatives there while others, having experienced intolerance and persecution in their homelands for years, feel that only in Palestine will they be welcomed and find peace and quiet and be given an opportunity to live and work.

The Immigration Act of 1924 and its "national origins" provisions posed other difficulties. Quotas, based on the census figures of 1910, limited immigration to 150,000 per year; of these, the major number of entry visas was reserved for immigrants of English, Irish, and German extraction. Applicants from Southern and Eastern Europe found the quotas inadequate, as did most of the displaced Jews who came from Central Europe, Poland, and the Baltic states.

The Displaced Persons Act of 1948, allowing an additional 100,000 annually for four years, did not solve this problem; but it helped all European D.P.'s of varied national, cultural, religious, and ethnic origins.

The choice of Palestine by the Jewish D.P.'s was dictated by stark realism and the desperate wish for survival. The refugees knew that the virus of anti-Semitism had infected the very body of Europe. They were themselves the survivors of Dachau and Bergen-Belsen and Buchenwald. For them the future as well as the present was perilous anywhere but in Palestine. In the D.P. camps, they received the grim tidings of the Kielce pogroms (1946) in Poland and of hostility in every nation of Europe. They wanted the chance to begin new lives in a new land, where they could be part of a self-respecting community and live again as human beings with dignity. They wanted to rebuild a nation and themselves — and be healed in the act.

But a new tragedy faced these stateless Jews: though World War II had ended, though democracy had vanquished dictatorship, the gates of Palestine were closed.

Why were Jewish refugees unable to enter Palestine at the end of World War II?

In the spring of 1939, the British government published a White Paper announcing a new policy for Palestine.

This document, issued by Colonial Secretary Malcolm MacDonald on behalf of Neville Chamberlain's cabinet, set a maximum figure of 75,000 for Jewish immigration in the following five years, at the rate of 10,000 per year, with 25,000 additional for refugees from Nazism. Jewish immigration to Palestine was to cease in 1944 unless the Arabs acquiesced in it. The Jews were thus to be reduced to a permanent minority in the Jewish National Home, frozen at about one-third of the population.

In addition, the White Paper limited the right of Jewish colonists to purchase land for reclamation and development to an area comprising only 5 per cent of Palestine. Within ten years, an Arab state in Palestine was to be set up, for the Arabs would remain a majority.

The 1939 White Paper was, in part, a British concession to Arab nationalists who, in 1936 and 1939, had rioted against Jewish immigration. The Chamberlain government, carrying out its ill-fated policy of appeasement, wooed the Arabs in hopes of winning their allegiance in case of war with Germany — a fruitless effort, as it turned out, for there was strong Arab sympathy for the Nazi cause.

In the House of Commons, Winston Churchill led in condemning the White Paper as "a plain breach of a solemn obligation" and as "another Munich."

In the United States and in many other countries, Christians and Jews protested this clear repudiation of the Balfour Declaration.

The Permanent Mandates Commission of the League of Nations declared the White Paper to be in contravention of the Palestine Mandate.

These protests were of no avail. The White Paper stood.

When World War II ended in 1945, thousands of Europe's surviving Jews were barred from entering Palestine and were forced to languish in the D.P. camps — homeless, penniless, despairing. Moved by their plight, President Truman urged Britain to allow at least 100,000 to enter Palestine.

After considerable discussion and some recrimination, Prime Minister Attlee responded by asking the American government to join with his government in an investigation of the Palestine problem by a joint Anglo-American Committee of Inquiry. The invitation was accepted by the United States government.

What was the Anglo-American Committee of Inquiry?

The Committee, appointed by Prime Minister Attlee and President Truman, was composed of six Britons and six Americans. Of these twelve men, the American public came to know well, from their lectures and books, British M.P. Richard H. S. Crossman, attorney Bartley C. Crum, and foreign affairs expert James G. McDonald (who in 1949 became the first U. S. Ambassador to Israel).

The Committee held its first hearings in Washington in January 1946. Later it proceeded to London, Cairo, Jerusalem, and various Arab capitals. It heard testimony reflecting many viewpoints: Zionist and anti-Zionist, binationalist and pro-Arab, anti-British and pro-American. Some of the Committee visited the D.P. camps in Germany and Austria and spoke with survivors of the Nazi terror. They heard at first hand the poignant pleas of Jews begging to be allowed to go to Palestine. In Palestine, they learned how British officials opposed Jewish colonization; they noted the astonishing progress of Jewish public health and education, agriculture and industry. They saw the transformation of desert and wasteland — constructive results which were beneficial to both Palestinian Arabs and Jews.

Four positive recommendations highlighted the Committee's report, issued on May 1, 1946:

(1) Admit 100,000 Jewish refugees from Europe during 1946 and allow further immigration according to the principles of the Palestine Mandate.

(2) Abrogate the land and immigration restrictions of the MacDonald White Paper.

(3) Until the United Nations establishes a new trusteeship for Palestine, reaffirm the League of Nations Mandate with the obligation to facilitate Jewish immigration and colonization in Palestine.

(4) Reject the principle that Jewish immigration must be subject to Arab consent.

In dealing with "Refugee Immigration Into Palestine," the report stated:

> We know of no country to which the great majority can go in the immediate future other than Palestine. Furthermore, that is where almost all of them want to go. . . . We believe it is essential that they should be given an opportunity to do so at the earliest possible time.

But the Anglo-American Committee report was not implemented by Foreign Secretary Bevin and Prime Minister Attlee. The American government had no authority in the matter and could do nothing on its own.

Impatience among both the Jewish D.P.'s in Europe and the Palestinian Jews increased — and tension rose.

What caused the growth of terrorism in Palestine?

For nearly all of the Jews of Europe, the issue was either life in Palestine or death. For the Jews of Palestine, it was liberty or death.

Though Dr. Chaim Weizmann deplored terrorism and though the 1946 World Zionist Congress in Basle condemned it, the circumstances which gave rise to extremism became steadily worse. The Zionists had warned that, if British military action against the Jews continued and if refugees were prevented from finding haven in the National Home, Jewish youth would continue to fight to save their fellow Jews and bring them to safety in Palestine. The warning was dramatized by the growth of *Irgun Zvai Leumi* (National Military Organization) and the Stern Group ("Fighters for the Freedom of Israel"). These were relatively small separatist organizations, to be distinguished from the Haganah, the legitimate Jewish self-defense movement. Haganah remained the dominant element despite provocation both by the terrorist groups and by the British.

The *Irgun*, led by Menahem Beigin, warned occupants to evacuate British military and public buildings before they were bombed; but the Stern group seldom gave warning to the British "alien conquerors on Jewish soil." The terrorists, intent on forcing the British out of Palestine, had learned some of their techniques from both Arabs and British; for the Arabs had assaulted new Jewish settlements in 1920 and had attacked Jerusalem, Haifa, and Hebron in 1929, while British soldiers, experienced in commando tactics from World War II, often turned to repressive methods in their treatment of the Palestinian Jews. The Haganah, whose membership included thousands of Palestinian Jews who had fought valiantly in North Africa and Europe with the British army, resisted courageously.

It was not the terrorists who ultimately forced the British out of Palestine. The decisive factors were:

(1) The pressure of unauthorized immigrants, 57,000 of whom were kept in British detention centers at one time on Cyprus.

(2) The passive resistance and non-cooperation of the Palestinian Jewish community.

(3) Its refusal to be cowed by the British military, as at the time of the wholesale arrest of Jewish Agency leaders in 1946.

(4) Various forms of military resistance by the Haganah not involving loss of life, such as blowing up communications and British radar stations used to locate immigrant ships.

(5) Resistance to armed searches in villages and settlements.

CHAPTER FOUR

Zion Reborn

Why did the British submit the Palestine problem to the United Nations?

Most British administrators in Palestine looked upon the Zionist enterprise as both futile and vexatious. Some government elements in London were more sympathetic. Between the two groups, colonial and domestic, there was a deep-rooted conflict. This was echoed in the growing bitterness between the Jews and Arabs, each of whom felt themselves alternately befriended and betrayed by the British.

In truth, for almost two and a half decades the British had wavered between the two peoples, unable to reconcile the apparent alternatives: Strangle the Zionist movement in Palestine? Or allow the returning Jews to occupy their ancient land and thus risk armed resistance by Arabs fired with a newly awakened political enthusiasm? The British would have preferred a policy of divide and rule. But both Arab and Jewish communities were conscious national entities opposed to permanent tutelage.

Finally, nettled by world-wide criticism of its footless policy in Palestine, harassed by Jewish resistance, and weakened by economic crisis at home, the British government handed the problem over to the United Nations in February of 1947.

In this abrupt move, the Mandatory may have hoped to frighten the Jews by the announcement of its readiness to leave the country. The British may have looked for a United Nations combination of Soviet and Moslem states, plus several Dominions and some Latin American and Central American states, to defeat proposals for a permanent solution. They may have thought that the United States, alarmed by potential Soviet exploitation of the situation, would lead in inviting Britain to reassume the Mandate. If such were the motives of the British, they were based on false hopes. But this no one could have known when the General Assembly appointed the United Nations Special Committee on Palestine — UNSCOP — to investigate the entire Palestine problem and make recommendations toward a solution.

What was the United Nations Special Committee on Palestine?

UNSCOP, appointed in May 1947, included eleven "middle powers" and smaller nations: Australia, Canada, Czechoslovakia, Guatemala, Holland, India, Iran, Peru, Sweden, Uruguay, and Yugoslavia. Its report, prepared after three months of investigation in Europe, Palestine, and the Arab states, listed eleven unanimous recommendations, the most important of which emphasized the need (1) to terminate the Mandate at the earliest practicable date; (2) to preserve the "economic unity of Palestine as a whole"; and (3) to safeguard "the sacred character of the Holy Places."

As for the political future of the country, there were majority and minority opinions. A minority of three — India, Iran, and Yugoslavia — recommended a unified central state. The majority group — with the exception of Australia, which abstained — recommended three distinct political units: a Jewish state, an Arab state, and an international regime for Jerusalem and environs. The two new states would be called upon to adopt constitutions and sign a treaty of economic union.

The main contribution of UNSCOP's majority finding was the recognition of the existence in Palestine of two distinct national groups, Jewish and Arab, each with legitimate rights to independence and unwilling to be subordinated to the other. The answer reached was a recommendation to give each group independence in a limited area and to require both groups to co-operate peacefully in their mutual interest.

Two human factors played a significant part in the composition of this historic report.

First was the *Exodus 1947* incident. Under the auspices of Haganah, a former Chesapeake Bay steamer, the *President Warfield*, arrived in Palestine with 4,500 European refugees after a battle at sea with a British cruiser and three destroyers. These 4,500 refugees were forcibly returned to Port de Bouc, France, their port of embarkation, and then sent to camps in Germany.

The second was the visit made by a subcommittee of UNSCOP to D.P. camps in Europe, where the hopelessness and homelessness of the D.P.'s who wanted to go to Palestine confirmed the findings of the 1946 Anglo-American Committee of Inquiry.

On September 25, 1947, the UNSCOP report was submitted to the General Assembly. After extensive revisions, the majority view was adopted at a historic session on November 29, 1947. The vote was 33 for, 13 against. The United States and the Soviet Union both voted for partition.

Did the United States use pressure to secure adoption of the UNSCOP proposals to partition Palestine?

The United States did not take the initiative in supporting UNSCOP's majority partition plan, and in fact adopted a policy of repeated delay until the final days before the vote.

Although the President and the Congress favored partition, there were strong elements in the State Department, in direct charge of American policy on Palestine, which tried to defeat the plan. President Truman played an active role only after being apprised of the disparity between his own pledges and the instructions given to the American U.N. delegation by the State Department.

The State Department's hostility to Jewish statehood was not dispelled by passage of the partition resolution. Three and a half months later — in March of 1948 — this enmity was revealed when the U.N. delegation suddenly reversed its position and advocated a U.N. trusteeship for Palestine — a move rendered futile by the failure of the General Assembly to adopt it and by the termination of the British Mandate on May 14, 1948, followed immediately by the proclamation of Israel statehood in accord with the U.N. partition plan.

Smaller nations had undoubtedly been impressed in the autumn of 1947 by the evident confidence of the big powers — who had such a stake in the stability of the Middle East — that partition would be the best solution. The greatest influence was the prospect of settling a major problem with an agreement between the United States and the USSR — for the Soviet Union, despite its long-time antagonism to Zionism, had expressed approval of partition in the spring of 1947; and shortly thereafter the United States announced its support. Although Great Britain abstained, other members of the British Commonwealth — Australia, Canada, New Zealand, and the Union of South Africa — voted for partition.

The Arabs succeeded in winning over some of the states normally regarded as securely within the United States voting column. A number of Latin American nations generally considered amenable to United States influence voted against partition. Had the American delegation exerted pressure, these nations would have felt impelled to vote, with the United States, for partition.

This democratic procedure of exchanging opinions and abiding by a two-thirds majority vote on a substantive issue on the U.N. agenda did not, however, deter the Arab nations. They condemned the U.N. for the partition decision and vowed to fight it — a promise which they kept on May 15, 1948, when five member states of the Arab League invaded Palestine.

Why did the Arab armies invade the new state of Israel?

Israel accepted the U.N. partition decision, believing it would guarantee peace, freedom, and self-determination for both the Jews and the Palestinian Arabs. Although the Jews had been promised Palestine under the Balfour Declaration, they accepted the compromise · of partition in the hope that its endorsement by the U.N. would mean peaceful implementation. But the Arabs rejected it and sent military units into Palestine to harass lines of communication and attack Jewish settlements in an effort to prevent partition. Such warfare by Arab irregulars and Arab armies had been predicted during the U.N. debates on Palestine by Jamal el-Husseini of the Palestine Arab Higher Committee: "The partition line proposed shall be nothing but a line of blood and fire."

When Britain withdrew from Palestine, the political leadership of the five Arabic-speaking countries of Egypt, Transjordan, Syria, Iraq, and Lebanon welcomed the opportunity for a *Jihad,* a holy war, to destroy the new Jewish state. The facts seemed to indicate to the Arabs that, without British defense forces or a U.N. police force, the Jews could not protect themselves against the armed forces of the five Arab states. The Arabs were 25,000,000 people, while the Jews in Palestine were only 650,000. The Arab armies were equipped with modern weapons of warfare, some of which came from the British. They felt that the campaign would be brief — a few days or, at the most, a few weeks. The Arab armies would "drive the Jews into the sea"; and then the Jewish farms and villages, cattle and chickens, homes and shops would be theirs.

The keynote was sounded in a BBC broadcast by Abdur-Raham Azzam Pasha, then secretary-general of the Arab League: "This will be a war of extermination and a momentous massacre which will be spoken of like the Mongolian Massacres and the Crusades."

The Arab spokesmen seemed to believe their own propaganda. For with little preparation, with scant co-ordination among the Arab armies, with no solidarity beyond their press releases and, most important of all, without the elemental morale required for any army, the Arabs undertook a war against the Israelis. After bitter fighting throughout 1948, the Arabs were driven back and defeated by the determined soldiers of the new state, whose slogan had been, as in many times past, *"Ain brerah* — no alternative."

Of prime importance was the superior technological resourcefulness of those European Jews who had fought underground in the Haganah against the British — and above ground in the Jewish Brigade of the British army against the Germans.

ISRAELI SOLDIERS IN FRONT OF MOVIE HOUSE IN TEL AVIV

What about atrocities in the Arab-Israeli war?

War itself is the worst atrocity. As in every war, so in the Arab-Israel conflict, there were many accusations of atrocities.

A "pre-state" war had been launched by Mufti-directed gangs who had a long record of terrorism dating back to 1920. On November 30, 1947, the day after the U.N. partition vote, eight Jews were killed by Arabs. In December 1947, Arabs beat and stabbed to death near Haifa forty-one Jews, employees of the Consolidated Refineries Ltd. In March 1948, thirteen Jews were killed in an explosion at the Jewish Agency building in Jerusalem. In the Old City, the Arab Legion destroyed twenty-seven synagogues, burning the holy scrolls and sacred vessels.

British soldiers were closely linked with Arab terrorists. On February 1, 1948, several of them blew up the *Palestine Post* building in Jerusalem, injuring twenty persons, four of whom later died.

On February 2, 1948, buildings on Ben Yehuda Street in Jerusalem were blown up. Fifty-two Jews were killed and hundreds injured. The evidence pointed to the British, but Arab "commandos" claimed credit.

On April 13, 1948, a tragic event occurred when a convoy of doctors and nurses of the Hadassah Hospital, accompanied by professors of the Hebrew University, were on their way to Mount Scopus. They were unarmed, traveling in ambulances clearly marked as non-military vehicles. Advance notice had been given to both British and Arabs. The convoy was ambushed by the Arabs while British soldiers — still responsible under the Mandate for the preservation of law and order — stood by immobile. Seventy-seven doctors, nurses, and professors were killed or burned to death.

The Israelis were also not without fault. In the days of the Mandate there had been violent reactions to British rule — the bombing of the King David Hotel in 1946, the Acre Prison break, and the booby-trapped bodies of the hanged British sergeants in 1947. But their most deplorable atrocity took place in Deir Yassin, invaded by the Irgun and Stern groups on April 9, 1948. The Irgun's amplifiers warned the population of Deir Yassin to leave, for the village would be attacked at a specific time, and Arab terrorists hiding there would be asked to give an accounting. At the time specified, the Irgun invaded the village and shot 250 of the inhabitants. This ruthless deed was bitterly condemned by responsible Jewish leaders.

The deplorable assassination of Count Bernadotte — which Israel condemned and for which Israel paid a substantial indemnity — is still unsolved; but it seems to have been a Sternist Act, for an offshoot of that group, "The Fatherland Front," boasted of the act.

28

Were Holy Places desecrated by the Israelis and is access denied to pilgrims?

Incidents of desecration did undoubtedly occur during the fighting in 1948. This was inevitable — as any review of the European wars of the past centuries will disclose.

Some of the monasteries, built in ancient days like fortresses, had been occupied by the British military during the Mandatory period and later were turned over by them to the Arabs. In subsequent attacks these places suffered damage. It should be recalled that, during World War II, the American military similarly found it necessary to send the air force to blast to rubble the Monte Cassino Abbey in Italy.

The total damage to religious institutions in Israel was comparatively small. Damage and looting did take place, but not as much as occurred in other countries during wartime or during agitated periods of social stress. Cases of unauthorized interference with and violation of church property did occur in the areas of actual warfare, mostly where buildings changed hands twice and sometimes three times a day.

The Israel government enacted a program of repairs for church buildings and other ecclesiastical property damaged during the war, particularly the Roman Catholic Church of the Dormition which, along with the rest of the city of Jerusalem, underwent continuous bombardment by the Arab Legion. Israel alone assumed these heavy responsibilities in spite of the fact that the war with the surrounding Arab states was not of Israel's making. Repairs were carried out by the Department of Public Works and funds supplied by the Ministry of Religions.

During the first months of Israel's statehood, when many of the ecclesiastical centers were located in military zones, the clergy complained that freedom of movement was restricted. Restrictions were then lifted and the clergy granted the same freedom of movement enjoyed by the average Israeli citizen. The clergy are actually privileged, for arrangements have been made to enable priests and ministers to enter the Old City of Jerusalem and return at will into Israeli territory.

The Jews of Israel have filed a complaint of similar nature. They are forbidden access to the Wailing Wall, historic site of Israel's lamentation of the Temple's destruction in 70 A.D., despite international guarantees that it would be made accessible to them and rendered inviolate.

29

CHAPTER FIVE

By the Sweat of Thy Brow

What was the outcome of the Arab-Israeli war?

By the early weeks of 1949, when Acting U.N. Mediator Dr. Ralph Bunche was negotiating armistice agreements, four factors had emerged:

(1) *The new state of Israel was firmly established.* The Israelis had taken up where the British Mandatory had left off, organized the machinery of government, provided housing and employment for a steady flow of refugees from Europe, and appeared before the Security Council as a sovereign state.

(2) *The Army of Israel had proved its effectiveness.* It had successfully repelled the armies of Egypt, Syria, Iraq, Lebanon, and Transjordan.

(3) *The Arab world had suffered a major military and political defeat.* This defeat revealed long-standing weaknesses within the Arab states and led to numerous changes — but unfortunately no substantial reforms. Disclosures of corruption, bribery, and nepotism resulted in the overthrow of ruling groups in Lebanon and Iraq and in the establishment of the dictatorships of Zayim (later assassinated) and Shishekly in Syria and of Naguib in Egypt. In 1951, King Abdullah of Jordan was assassinated. The following year King Farouk fled from Cairo. By 1953, no Arab state participating in the Arab-Israel war was governed by the same clique.

● (4) *The authority of the United Nations had, with qualified success, been established.* The Acting U.N. Mediator set the armistice at points that increased the partition area by approximately 100 miles beyond the original 6500 square miles. Eventually Jordan annexed the Old City of Jerusalem and the remaining portion of Arab Palestine, while Egypt assumed control of the Gaza strip. In creating the Palestine Conciliation Commission and the Mixed Armistice Commissions, the U.N. admitted that unsettled problems would continue to require surveillance and negotiation. Most disturbing of the problems were the plight of almost 600,000 Arabs who fled from Israel and, as refugees, became U.N. wards; the status of Jerusalem; and the border clashes, particularly along the Jordan-Israel boundary. ●

How did Israel adjust to the 125% increase of population during the first five years of statehood?

To the people of Israel, the rapid population increase was the fulfillment of the hope and pledge in the Israel Proclamation of Independence: "The State of Israel will be opened to the immigration of Jews from all the countries of their dispersion." They were not surprised that in the little more than thirty months from Israel's establishment in 1948 until the end of 1950, 510,034 Jewish immigrants came to Israel's shores — 26,000 more than the 484,000 who had come to Palestine during the previous thirty years.

This phenomenal Ingathering of the Exiles brought counsel from friends in other lands to slacken the pace. To such advice, Prime Minister David Ben-Gurion replied: "It was for this that Israel was established, and it is by virtue of this alone that it will stand."

The fabric of this swiftly growing society was strained by the heterogeneity of the immigrants, notably the several hundred thousand Oriental Jews who came from Iraq, North Africa, and Yemen. In the thirty years prior to 1948, four-fifths of Jewish immigrants had come from Europe; after 1948, less than one-half came from Europe, the greater number from Asia and Africa. Pioneer families, inconvenienced by this vast immigration, nevertheless approved of the basic tenet of the Law of the Return, promulgated in July of 1950: "Every Jew has the right to immigrate to Israel."

A difficult adjustment was necessary in the economic sphere. The Israel of 1948 had only meager natural resources, limited capital, and no friendly states on its borders. The housing of this extraordinarily large immigration would have been more difficult if it had not been for the fact that some Arab villages were left vacant when their owners needlessly fled the country, thus providing accommodations for about one-fourth of the Jewish immigrants.

Most of the 750,000 newcomers were impoverished and unskilled. Some were illiterate. Many were diseased, old and infirm, lame or blind. Almost all had to be housed and fed first in "tent city" reception centers, later in work villages. At the same time they had to be given medical care and trained for some kind of job — all at public expense. The enormous cost inevitably brought about a drastic lowering of the standard of living in Israel; for only part of the expense could be defrayed by the United Jewish Appeal in the United States. The greatest sacrifice was made by the Israelis, but their fellow Jews in other parts of the world felt a compelling moral obligation to aid them in the development of one of the world's newest republics.

Is Israel a democratic state?

Politically, economically, and socially, Israel is a modern democracy. Israel grants full citizenship privileges and the right to vote to every citizen above eighteen years of age — man and woman, Jew and Arab, Christian, Moslem and Druse. Under the recently adopted Women's Equal Rights Law, there is complete equality before the law between men and women.

Israel's parliament, the Knesset, is a unicameral legislative body of 120 members — including eight Arabs — chosen by popular vote, with proportional representation. The cabinet is responsible to the Knesset and stays in office only as long as it commands a majority.

The judiciary — an independent body, as in the United States — protects the citizen against arbitrary use of government power. The judicial process is accessible to all citizens.

There is freedom of speech and assembly, and freedom of press and publication.

There is freedom of culture. Arabs conduct their schools in Arabic, and the Arabic language is recognized for all purposes. Arab members of the Knesset address that body in their own language. Similarly, though Hebrew is the official language, immigrants are free to publish newspapers and books in the languages of their countries of origin, and many make use of this right.

Israel's economic democracy is reflected in social and economic forms which vary from free enterprise to agricultural collectives and consumers' cooperatives. There are four main types of agricultural settlements: (1) the *moshava,* where settlers own property and farm on a private basis; (2) the *moshav ovdim,* where farmers own their own farms, but where buying and selling is co-operatively organized and hired labor is discouraged; (3) the *kibbutz* (or *kvutza*), where all property is owned communally and the family is a social but not an economic unit; (4) the *moshav shitufi,* a growing group representing a compromise between the *moshav ovdim* and the *kibbutz.* Histadrut, the General Federation of Jewish Workers, provides many social services such as housing, health measures, unemployment relief, immigrant resettlement, old-age security, and vocational training.

Under the unified, state-controlled Educational Act, schooling is assured for every child, Jew or Arab, under fourteen.

Israel, like the most advanced nations, is not perfect. But it is a democracy in its concern for the human personality, its political liberties, its independent judiciary, its educational system, and its effort to achieve equality of opportunity for all. Its inspiration comes both from the Western world and from the vision and ethical imperatives of the ancient Hebrew prophets.

Is Israel a theocracy?

Theocracy, the government of a state by a religious group claiming divine authority, does not prevail in Israel. Israel is a democracy where supreme authority resides in an elected parliament, and where law is thus under popular control.

The laws of Israel assure complete freedom of worship and conscience to all — Jew, Moslem, Christian, Druse. People have free choice — to believe or not to believe, to worship or not to worship. But rabbis of Reformed Judaism have yet to attain accredited status within the Jewish religious community where Orthodox Jewry is firmly in control.

Variation in religious affiliations in Israel is as wide as in America. Among the Jews there are the very orthodox, who would like to establish Judaism as a state religion, to impose dietary laws, and to revive the Sanhedrin of Biblical times. The degree of conformity descends the scale to the indifferent and the agnostics. The bulk of the population is religious by habit and upbringing but with varying degrees of observance.

Some of the intensely religious have formed political groups which at the last elections polled about 12 per cent of the votes. Thus they were able to secure sufficient political strength in the coalition government to demand retention of those procedures for the regulation of marriage and divorce which prevailed under the Turkish and British regimes and which placed these aspects of personal law under the control of religious courts — rabbinical, Moslem, and canonical, according to community affiliation.

Similarly they insisted that meat rations in Jewish areas be kosher. There are some other provisions which have aroused opposition in certain quarters, just as "Blue Laws" have been a source of irritation and contention in many communities in America.

The average Israeli is amazed at the occasional alarm expressed in the United States that Israel will be overwhelmed either by religious fanaticism or by lack of religion. The Israelis know that they are in danger neither of a theocratic regime nor of atheism. They have a faith, a deeply religious faith which assumes unconventional forms in the *kibbutzim* and which may seem secular in contrast to conventional patterns of organized religion; but it is expressed in new ways so that holidays like Passover and Purim take on a religious significance with patriotic overtones. For the Bible, the Israelis retain a deep, abiding love; and belief in God is as prevalent as in any other Western land.

What are Israel's major problems today?

Among the many problems facing Israel, three demand immediate attention:

(1) *Peace in the Middle East.* Israel cannot enjoy territorial security so long as border incidents continue and the Arab states, planning a "second round," refuse to negotiate a permanent peace. Efforts to develop a sound economy are crippled when human and material resources must be devoted to building defenses and maintaining strong armed forces, while also coping with an economic boycott by the Arab League. Peace is no less important to the Arab states, for the basic problems of the Middle East — retarded development, poverty, illiteracy, and disease — cannot be solved unless there is full-scale co-operation throughout the region. Moreover, the tragic plight of Arab refugees deeply concerns the Israelis; the Israelis want to contribute to the solution of that problem, thus setting a pattern in understanding toward their neighbors. They have made concrete offers of assistance, realizing that the absence of peace endangers the security of a region of tremendous strategic importance to the defense of the free world.

(2) *A stable, independent economy.* Israel seeks to develop a normal, healthy economy, making productive workers out of immigrants, providing adequate housing, developing mineral resources, reclaiming saline soil, irrigating arid lands, planning cities and towns with care, and maintaining high cultural levels. This depends in considerable measure on skilled professional and technological personnel from the West, but their aid is not easily available in a land where comforts are few and financial security not assured. Furthermore, Israel today suffers from an unfavorable trade balance and a fluctuating exchange. The government is forced to import about 78 cents worth of goods for every 22 cents exported.

(3) *Cultural integration.* The face of Israel today is the face of the world. Its citizens, who come from virtually every part of the globe, speak in many tongues and present a rich, rare tapestry of the human race with mingled Oriental and Occidental motifs. They need now a balanced, truly representative society, with an indigenous Israel culture which will retain both the moral fiber of the Jewish religion and the universality of Jewish culture over the past two thousand years. In dealing with this question, Mrs. Golda Myerson, Israel's Minister of Labor, has said: "Here is the problem: the cultural problem — how to make one people out of all these different tribes — how to mold them into one cultured people."

To solve such problems, the Israelis look to themselves; but they have received encouragement and aid from Jewish communities throughout the free world and especially from the United States.

Has Israel received more financial assistance than the Arab states?

Both Israel and the Arab states have received financial assistance based upon need and upon their readiness and ability to use that assistance.

For instance, Israel submitted specific development projects with requests for loans to the U. S. Export-Import Bank. It subsequently received two loans amounting to $135,000,000.

The Arab states neither formulated such programs nor requested such loans. Indeed, they have often asserted they do not need or desire American financial assistance. Syria, which has extensive underdeveloped areas, has refused Point Four assistance. Some $64,000,000 earmarked for Arab refugees by the Mutual Security Program lies still untouched for want of sound development projects.

Fortunately, this negative attitude is changing. President Mohammed Naguib has requested and has received increased Point Four funds for Egypt.

Through the remarkable generosity of Jews in America and throughout the world, Israel has received considerable sums in recent years to help absorb its 750,000 refugees. Supplementary funds for industrial and commercial expansion have been provided by the sale of Israel Bonds.

On behalf of Arab refugees, no such response has been forthcoming from Arab sources or from Arab sympathizers — although similar resources are available to the Arab states. Arabs abroad, as well as oil-rich and land-wealthy Arabs in the Middle East, could contribute large amounts of money.

In Arab nations, foreign capital investments could be welcomed, instead of discouraged. Many business interests have, until recently, withdrawn from Egypt because of severe restrictions on foreign capital. Only the oil-producing areas (excepting Iran) have utilized sizeable outside investments to the extent of $2,000,000,000. Oil royalties, now exceeding $350,000,000 annually, could be used to develop the Arab lands.

In various foreign-aid appropriations, the U. S. Congress has allotted comparable funds to Israel and to the Arab states for refugee relief and resettlement, because the total numbers of Jewish and Arab refugees are roughly the same. Israel has received $120,000,000, the Palestine Arab refugees $153,000,000. In addition, the Arab refugees have received additional aid from other member states of the U.N. and from private organizations.)

In short, aid and investment for Middle East countries are determined by needs and request; these change as conditions change. The entire Middle East gains when financial assistance is granted to underdeveloped countries.

CHAPTER SIX

Orphans of the Storm

What is the nature of the refugee problem in the Middle East?

There are two refugee problems that must be faced in the Middle East: that of the Jewish refugees and that of the Arab refugees. Indissolubly linked, they evolve from the same post-war situation.

The fall of Nazism left millions of homeless and stateless persons in Europe, several hundred thousand of whom were Jewish refugees in the D.P. camps. At the same time, in Arabic-speaking countries, persecutions made refugees of several hundred thousand Jews.

In the Arab war against Israel, many Arabs of Palestine became so terrified and confused — a terror and confusion encouraged by Arab leaders — that they fled, despite efforts by Israel authorities to restrain them. In all, about 600,000 left Israel territory.

In the next five years, Israel accepted some 750,000 Jewish refugees, almost half from Arabic-speaking countries. About 120,000, forced to abandon their property, came from Iraq, another 50,000 from Yemen. Still others, similarly stripped of nearly all their possessions, came from Syria, Egypt, and North Africa.

Thus the vacuum created in Israel by the exodus of Arab refugees was quickly filled by Jewish refugees; as a consequence, there are more than a million and a half Jewish and Arab refugees in Israel and its immediate vicinity. Half of these, the Jewish refugees, are being absorbed as well as possible by the struggling republic of Israel. The other half, the Arab refugees — some 870,000 by United Nations count — are pawns in the political maneuvers of Arab leaders who still hope for the downfall of Israel.

Some appeals for aid have implied that there is only an Arab refugee problem, enabling propagandists to blame the Arab refugee plight on Israel. If proper attention is called to both Jewish and Arab refugee problems, much ill-will may be avoided and genuine human need, regardless of race or creed, will be served.

10/PS.

District Police Headquarters,
(C.I.D.)
P.O.B. 700.
Haifa.

26th April, 1948.

S E C R E T

A/A.I.G., C.I.D.

Subject:- General Situation - Haifa District.

Haifa remains quiet. Yesterday produced a noticeable change
in the general atmosphere and businesses and shops in the lower
town were open for the first time in many days. Traffic started
to move normally around the town and people returning to their
places of business filled the streets. In fact, Haifa presented
a more normal appearance than it had done for a long while.
Some Arabs were seen moving among the Jews in the lower town and
German Colony area and these were allowed free and unmolested
passage. An appeal has been made to the Arabs by the Jews to reopen their shops and businesses in order to relieve the difficulties
of feeding the Arab population. Evacuation was still going on
yesterday and several trips were made by 'Z' craft to Acre. Roads,
too, were crowded with people leaving Haifa with their belongings.
At a meeting yesterday afternoon Arab leaders reiterated their
determination to evacuate the entire Arab population and they have
been given the loan of ten 3-ton military trucks as from this
morning to assist the evacuation.

Yesterday morning a Jew attempted to pass the drop barrier of
Police H.Q. facing Palmers Gate wheeling a barrow. He was shot
and killed by a Police sentry.

At 0640 hrs. yesterday Tireh village was again attacked with
mortar fire. Casualties and damage not known.

A report has been received from Military to the effect that
at 23.50 hrs. yesterday Jews attacked Acre from the direction of
Ein Hamifratz and Tall al Fukhkhar. An advance party succeeded in
demolishing three houses in the Manshiya Quarter and then heavy
mortar fire was directed at the town. Several mortar bombs landed
in Acre Prison and all the inmates have escaped. The British warden
staff are safe. Military proceeded to the scene and opened fire
with artillery on Ein Hamifratz. The Jews thereupon withdrew and
a convoy of 11 vehicles was seen proceeding in the direction of
Haifa. Casualties to both sides are not known.

(A.J. Bidmead.)
for SUPERINTENDENT OF POLICE.

Copy:- District Commissioner, Haifa.
Superintendent of Police, Haifa.
File.

REPORT FROM BRITISH POLICE HEADQUARTERS, HAIFA

What caused the flight of Arabs from Israel?

Toward the close of 1947, the Arab Higher Committee, headed by the former Mufti of Jerusalem, Haj Amin el Husseini, began a double-edged propaganda campaign which resulted in a mass exodus of Arabs from Israel. On the one hand, the Committee predicted that the Haganah would engage in a campaign of terror against the Arabs. The reprehensible attack of the Irgun at Deir Yassin stirred some Arabs to hysteria, and the warnings from Arab radios to beware of future Deir Yassins helped to stimulate the flight from Palestine.

On the other hand, the Arab Higher Committee painted a glorious picture of what Palestinian life would be like after the Jews were driven into the sea by the triumphant Arab armies. They urged Arabs to evacuate their homes, thus leaving the field free for operations by the guerilla forces that began their attacks immediately after the U.N. partition vote of November 29, 1947.

At the same time the Arab League predicted a massacre of the Jews. The Arabs of Palestine, thus forewarned of a full-scale land, sea, and air invasion by their kinsmen, began to leave the land, confident of returning after a quick Arab victory. They left despite urgings by the Israeli government that they remain. (See the document reproduced on page 37.)

Normally, a plan to remove all Arabs from the Israel area to expedite the progress of mechanized armies would have been shrewd. But the strategy failed, for armistice lines, established by the U.N. Mediator and his staff, automatically placed the Arabs across a military boundary line and prevented their return.

During the Arab-Israeli war in 1948, Arab leaders would not allow their people to re-enter partitioned Palestine. But in 1949, after military defeat, these same Arab spokesmen reversed their stand. Now they sought to burden Israel's hard-pressed economy: they demanded immediate repatriation of Arab refugees to Israel and strict adherence to the 1947 partition plan against which they had fought so bitterly and which they had rendered ineffectual.

Some blame must be placed on the British Mandatory for its failure to preserve peace in the months preceding partition and for its encouragement of the Arab exodus. Then, too, some blame can be placed on the two terrorist groups in Israel which helped to stimulate panic among the Arabs. But the Arab refugee situation was created primarily by the forces which incited war in an attempt to prevent the partition of Palestine. If there had been no armed resistance to the U.N. partition plan, the exiled Arabs would be living in Israel today.

What is the present condition of Arab refugees?

1953 The United Nations lists 102,704 Arab refugees in Lebanon, 85,715 in Syria, nearly 475,000 in Jordan, and 207,632 in the Gaza Strip, now under Egyptian control. To the original 600,000 who left Palestine, a considerable number of newcomers, camp followers, and mendicants have been added. U.N. officials admit that the census figures are less than exact, for countless refugees register several times in the ration lines, while others are reluctant to relinquish the ration cards of deceased relatives.

Life in an Arab refugee camp is a shabby existence, debilitating and demoralizing, especially for those who left comfortable homes and established businesses or professions. The diet is far from adequate. Jobs are difficult to find in Jordan, barred by law in Egypt and Lebanon. For most Arab refugees, life in such camps is similar to the dreary existence they knew in the mud huts of squalid villages in Palestine or the existence still known today by many millions of Arabs — indigent villagers or Bedouins — who inhabit this depressed sector of the world.

There are a few bright spots. Medical facilities in the refugee camps have greatly lowered infant mortality, and schools available to refugee children have materially reduced illiteracy.

Although the Arab refugees represent less than 3 per cent of the world's estimated forty million refugees and have received more aid in money, food, clothing, and medicine than have the homeless of Korea, China, India, and Pakistan, they are surely not to be envied — for they live on an average of approximately $2.50 per month.

The Arab states have accepted little responsibility for the refugees. Their contributions for food, clothing, and housing have been scant. They have refused to resettle the refugees in the large Arab states which need farmers. They continue to demand the repatriation of these hapless people to Israel.

Israel has tried to treat its Arab population more equitably. After the armistice of 1949, there were 69,000 Arabs living in Israel. Now the number has increased to 175,000, as a result of the boundary adjustments, a reunion of families, and the legalizing of the entry of infiltrees. Israel cares for 19,000 Palestinian Arab refugees within its boundaries. It has agreed to make available frozen bank accounts to absentee Arabs and to make compensation for abandoned Arab lands — a genuine hardship for a nation feeling the stringency of foreign-exchange deficits.

In January 1952, the U.N. General Assembly voted a three-year project of $250,000,000, four-fifths for resettlement and $50,000,000 for relief — no permanent solution, but an admirable beginning.

How can the Arab refugee problem be solved?

(A prerequisite to any permanent settlement of the refugee problem is the establishment of peace between Israel and the Arab states. Israel has repeatedly pressed for such a peace, but the Arabs refuse because it would mean to them acknowledgment of a defeat they do not wish to accept as permanent.)To quote from the Fifth Progress Report of the United Nations Conciliation Commission, dated December 14, 1949:

> The Israel Delegation reaffirmed its desire to open direct peace nego-
> tiations with each of the interested parties. The Arab delegations de-
> clared that they "were not prepared to enter into direct negotiations
> with the representatives of Israel."

Meanwhile the Arab refugees, incited by agents of the Arab League and of the Communists, have become bitterly anti-U.N. and anti-U.S. Political agitators urge them to refuse resettlement in Arab lands. Yet it is unlikely that any sizeable number of Arab refugees will ever be repatriated to Israel. History is rarely reversed. The situation has changed as a result of the Arab-Israeli War of 1948. Israel has absorbed a large population; a new population and a new political entity have come into being. Have the Arabs any more likelihood of returning to Israel than the 13,000,000 Pakistani and Hindustani refugees to their previous habitats in partitioned India, or the 9,000,000 *Volksdeutsche* now in West Germany to their homes behind the Iron Curtain?

The solution for all these displaced peoples is resettlement in new lands. For the Arab refugees, resettlement should preferably be in the great under-populated areas of Iraq, Syria, and Jordan, where they can be integrated into societies with which they have ties of kinship, language, and tradition.

A broad resettlement program was proposed to the United Nations, in December 1951, by nineteen distinguished American church and civic leaders, including Bishop Charles K. Gilbert, Kenneth Scott Latourette, Archibald MacLeish, Reinhold Niebuhr, and James T. Shotwell. It envisaged an international fund of $800,000,000, to which Israel would make contribution by way of compensation for abandoned Arab lands. It called for a five-year U.N. program to develop the natural resources of the area.

The U.N. plan, establishing the $250,000,000 fund, was not so comprehensive, but it did incorporate the same basic principles. Already pilot projects are underway in Jordan and Lebanon.

Adjustments will have to be made for Arab lands abandoned in Israel, and for Jewish properties abandoned in Arab countries. But peace is an indispensable prerequisite.

What is the condition of Arabs in Israel?

Israel's Proclamation of Independence promised social and political equality to all of its citizens, regardless of faith. Arabs who remained in the country became full citizens. Moreover, most of the Arab refugees who have returned to Israel, whether legally or not, have been granted full citizenship rights. Certain military strategic border areas are still under military government. Many Arabs live in areas where security considerations call for certain restrictions applying to Arab and Jew alike, but such restrictions, principally on movement into or outside the areas, are gradually being lifted.

In Israel's first elections, some 30,000 Arabs were eligible to vote. Three Arab deputies were elected to the first Knesset. In the second election, in 1951, about 70,000 Arabs voted and eight were elected to the Knesset.

Arabic is an official language in the Knesset, in government publications, and in radio broadcasts of *Kol Israel*, the Voice of Israel. It is the language of instruction in the Arab public schools maintained by the Israel government. Attendance at school is compulsory for all children under fourteen. Today 90 per cent of Arab children attend school as against 45 per cent prior to the establishment of Israel.

The Israel government has helped to reorganize religious facilities for its Moslem citizens. There are now more than two hundred Moslem religious officials paid by the Israel government or out of the proceeds of Wakf (Moslem religious funds) administration. The Ministry of Religious Affairs employs a number of Moslem officials on its permanent staff and has set up a special section for the preservation of Moslem religious buildings.

The Arabs publish their own newspapers, ranging from right to left politically and all enjoying freedom of the press. The Israel government has been more tolerant of abusive statements in Arab publications than of similar attacks in the papers and magazines of Jewish extremists, for it has sedulously sought to avoid the charge of discrimination.

The government and Histadrut, Israel's Federation of Labor, have helped the Arabs establish more than fifty consumer and producer co-operatives, as well as several loan societies. They have increased the number of public clinics and hospitals and augmented Arab health services.

Arab women participate in communal and political affairs, casting their ballots on election days. Compulsory free education is reducing illiteracy among Arab girls. Israel's example in these respects has undoubtedly had considerable influence on the status of women in other Arab lands.

CHAPTER SEVEN

Lights and Shadows in the Arab World

Has the United States lost the friendship of the Arab world?

It is questionable whether Arab friendship for the United States has ever been anything more than the traditional deference of smaller nations toward a great power. The average Arab admires and yet dislikes the West, mostly because he uses the West as a gauge of his own success and failure.

The record of Arab amity in World War I was made clear by David Lloyd George, who, in writing about the peace treaties, noted that "most of the Arab races fought throughout the war for their Turkish oppressors. Arabia was the only exception in that respect. The Palestinian Arabs fought for the Turkish rule."

During World War II, Arab leaders, some of whom have of late been abusive of the United States and the West, were equally vocal as partisans of Hitler. In 1941, when British fortunes were at their lowest ebb, there was an open revolt in Iraq against the Allies — a revolt which had to be suppressed by British force.

Only Jordan, then under a British Mandate, joined in declaring war on Germany in 1939. The other Arab states did not declare war until Germany's defeat was imminent. To qualify for the U.N. charter conference in San Francisco, Egypt's declaration came on February 25, 1945, followed by Syria on February 27, Lebanon on February 28 and Saudi Arabia on March 2.

Israel is usually cited as the cause for Arab hostility toward the United States. But even if Israel did not exist, the Arabs would still have an argument for animus toward the West over oil concessions in Iran and Iraq, over the presence of British troops in the Suez, over Britain's continued influence in Jordan, Libya, and the Sudan.

The possibility of the Arab states' joining the Soviet bloc — a frequently voiced fear — appears most unlikely. Could Arab leaders seriously contemplate political suicide — an alliance which would inevitably lead to the overthrow of their feudal regimes?

What is the significance of the Arab League?

The Arab League — a loose political association of eight Arab states, Egypt, Jordan, Syria, Lebanon, Iraq, Libya, Saudi Arabia, and Yemen — has no effective authority and has not resolved even minor differences among its members, still less imposed needed reforms on the economies and political structures of those lands. It speaks of a "second round," yet laments the ignominious defeat suffered in the Arab-Israeli war of 1948, which revealed the internal disunity and corruption in the Arab governments of Egypt, Iraq, and Syria. In the press, on the radio, and in the halls of the U.N., it attacks "American imperialism" and "British interference"; but it finds difficulties in naming its own constructive contributions in the troubled Middle East. Only on Zionism are the members of the League united. Their opposition to Britain is not even unanimous, for both Jordan and Iraq have close treaty ties with the British.

That Egypt is now a republic; that Syria has adopted a new constitution; and that Lebanon has extended the franchise to women — this has been the result, not of Arab League progress, but of internal upheavals and revolutions in each respective land. In Egypt, President Naguib's land reforms have yet to be implemented. Yemen is still a medieval citadel of superstition and slavery; Saudi Arabia is still a primitive patriarchy. Rivalries among the Arab states continue and schisms abound.

The Arab League, established toward the close of World War II, was the creation of British Foreign Secretary Anthony Eden. Before this, Britain had denied the concept of Arab unity and sought to prevent its realization. Later the British, weary of disputes among Arab leaders and would-be kings, sought to achieve some order in the Middle East by uniting the Arab states.

Eden expected the League eventually to become the nucleus of a British-oriented military organization; but that objective was negated by Arab jealousies born of dynastic rivalries and suspicions. British power then began to wane in the Middle East despite the Allied victory over Germany, and Whitehall had to look to African colonies for strategic position.

Today the Arab League — little more than a bargaining post in negotiations with the West — runs the risk of becoming a device for personal aggrandizement by political leaders in each country. Some describe it as an instrument for Egyptian hegemony over the Arab world, but at present it serves only the divergent interests of the several Arab states. To nationalist Arab leaders, Jordan is still suspect because of its subservience to Britain, and Lebanon because of its 51 per cent Christian population.

What democratic forces are to be found in the Arab world?

Democratic forces in the Arab world are few and they are weak. The achievement of higher standards of living and genuine democracy among the peoples of the Arab world is a desirable goal, but the prognosis is not too encouraging. In some parts of the Arab world, the first stirrings of discontent are reflected in a small number of progressive movements. This very discontent, if checked too rigorously by the old order, may break out in extremism of either right or left. Yet the example of Israel with its Western influence and its freedom from a heritage of feudalism, plus U.S. and U.N. technical assistance, may help in the democratization of the Middle East through peaceful evolution.

Unhappily, the Arab world today, slowly emerging from a semi-feudal society, resists democratic processes. The democratic structures — parliaments, etc. — are still largely facades. Its only politically self-conscious groups are found in the middle class, especially among the volatile student bodies in Damascus, Cairo, Beirut, and Bagdad. Strongest political emotions seem centered on the growing nationalism of Arab states, many of which are only now releasing themselves from colonial domination and developing a consciousness of their dignity as nations.

The Middle East is dominated by a combination of landed interests, usurious financiers, and military cabals. The vast foreign-owned oil enterprises are the sole industry of consequence in Saudi Arabia and Iraq. Only in Lebanon, Egypt, and Syria, and to a lesser extent in Jordan, is there both a mercantile bourgeoisie and the beginnings of industrial development.

The growing industrial working class is open to modern political ideas, but it will not necessarily develop in a democratic direction. Communism and neo-fascism are two formidable rivals to democracy.

Can the economic and political difficulties of the Middle East be resolved within a democratic framework? The Arab lands, underpopulated and economically backward, have no forms of private enterprise able to undertake long-range schemes. Admirable beginnings have been made in the soil reclamation and rehabilitation projects of the Near East Society, in Musa Bey Alami's refugee resettlement farms in the Jericho Valley, the U.N.'s technical assistance under the FAO, WHO, and UNESCO, and Faha Hussein's literacy program in Egypt. These beginnings emphasize, however, their enormous distance away from a healthy democracy. Democracy, as we think of it and as reflected in the Middle East by both Israel and Turkey, will not be easily realized in Arab lands.

School for Arab refugee children, Gaza strip

Is there possibility of permanent peace between Israel and the Arab states?

The present anti-Israel attitude of Arab political leadership, at least as publicly expressed, is so intransigent as to seem to offer little hope of a *rapprochement* between the Arab states and Israel. Some Arab leaders have, however, recognized in private the possibility of peace with Israel.

There is no insurmountable barrier to peace between the two peoples. No genuine conflict of interests — political, territorial, or ethnic — exists between tiny Israel, which has a population of 1,500,000, and the nine Arabic-speaking countries (including the Sudan, soon to achieve independence), which have territories 160 times as large and a population of more than 45,000,000.

The Israelis feel sufficiently strong militarily to withstand an Arab attack. Moreover, they are confident that if the Arab states are not aided by the West to engage in an arms race, there will be no "second round" of Arab aggression.

Both Israel and the Arab states are underdeveloped. They need not expand or covet their neighbors' borders to find *Lebensraum* for their populations. They do not vie for outlets on the sea, for Israel and most of the Arab states have such outlets; to Jordan, which does not, Israel has offered free port facilities at Haifa. Nor is there a necessity to compete for markets. Hundreds of thousands of potential customers live within their own borders. In addition, the economies of Israel and the Arab states can be so organized and developed as to complement each other.

Many cultural traditions are held in common. Though Israel has brought the Occident into the Middle East, the new state of Israel is an indigenous power in the region, working toward an amalgam of Occidental with Semitic culture and tradition. Even the Arabic and the Hebrew languages are cousin tongues.

There is therefore a large area of common interest which augurs well for the success of a permanent peace settlement. In years to come the goal will be the persuasion of the Arab leadership to take a realistic view of Israel — to recognize that Israel exists — to accept the fact that Israel can be neither denied nor destroyed, save by a catastrophe so far-reaching that it would wipe out the Arab states as well.

In 1953, Prime Minister David Ben-Gurion told a reporter of the New York *Herald Tribune*: "We are not seeking any military adventures. We want peace for several reasons. First, we want peace for its own sake. We know what war is like. Second, we need peace to build up the country and settle more immigrants. Third, we want to play our part in developing the whole area and bringing it to a better life."

Have the American people had the opportunity to hear the Arab point of view?

There has always been a powerful movement in the United States on behalf of the Arab interests. It has been expressed through a number of Americans with specialized interests in the Middle East: missionaries, YMCA workers, exchange professors, oil operators, mining engineers, *et al.* From the ranks of these specialists, the United States government has solicited much of its "expert" opinion on the area. While the government's public statements have at times been favorable to Israel, the actual implementation of policy has been the responsibility of civil servants trained in a tradition which from the outset has regarded Zionism with disfavor.

The Arab embassies and legations have sent representatives to service clubs, public forums, civic functions, and college seminars, and they have placed in the mails enormous quantities of anti-Israel material. Delegations of professors and scholars from Middle Eastern lands have gone beyond academic pursuits to tour the United States on behalf of a pro-Arab point of view. More than 1,500 Arab exchange students have made their voices heard.

Arab newsmen at the United Nations have not hesitated to present the Arab's anti-Israel point of view, as have delegations of Arab journalists brought here by the State Department as part of its cultural interchange program. Israel's voice at the U.N. is, at most, as one to six in meeting the attacks of the Arab nations, and as one to ten or twelve in countering the Arab-Asian bloc.

For a number of years, Arab speakers and literature were made available by the Arab Office in Washington and by the Institute of Arab-American Affairs in New York City. These efforts were supplemented by two short-lived organizations — by the Committee for Peace and Justice in the Holy Land and by HELP (the Holy Land Emergency Liaison Program). More recently, the American Friends of the Middle East has established regional offices with a propaganda program unsympathetic to Israel. Unfortunately, many of its sponsors have frequently been known as anti-Israeli.

A number of notorious anti-Semites like Allen Zoll, Gerald L. K. Smith, Robert Williams, Joseph Kamp, Upton Close, and Gerald Winrod, have offered their services to the Arab legations and U.N. delegations as pro-Arab, anti-Jewish propagandists; and in a number of instances, the offers have been accepted.*

---

* See *The Troublemakers*, by Arnold Forster and Benjamin R. Epstein (New York: Doubleday and Company, 1952).

47

*What are the views of Christian missionaries and educators of the
Middle East concerning Zionism and Israel?*

Many missionaries are unaware of the facts of Zionist aspirations and
Israel's achievements. Even among American educators in Middle East
institutions, there prevails an unfortunate, though understandable, disinclina-
tion to see Israel for themselves, lest their efforts to see "both sides of the
question" be misconstrued by their Arab constituents.

In view of Arab chauvinism and general distrust of the foreigner, perhaps
the Middle East missionary or educator could not be expected to show
sympathetic interest in Israel as a new creative force in a blighted area. In
a predominantly Moslem milieu, Christians from abroad must constantly
prove their loyalty to Arab aspirations. The acid test today is their opposition to Israel and a willingness to serve without attempting to convert Moslems to Christianity. To prove fidelity to the Arab cause, many a Middle
East educator will, on his periodic fund-raising tours in the United States,
speak critically of the new Jewish state. Support for missions often comes
from individuals associated with American business interests in Arab lands
and endowments from oil companies which prefer not to disturb the established order.

Many Middle East missionaries and educators are bound by their own
particular formula for the Christianizing of the Moslem world. They be-
lieved the Moslem world would be Christianized if an Arab nationalism
were aroused which would throw off the Turkish yoke and then be free to
embrace Christianity. The nationalism they helped to foment did not,
however, initiate a movement away from Islam; instead it precipitated its
revival. A new nationalism and an equally fanatical Islam, epitomized by
the reactionary Moslem Brothershood, arose to counter increased Western
influence in the Middle East. However, some missionaries and educators,
seeking to place the blame for their sincere but mistaken judgment of the
situation, place the sole blame upon Zionism for the failure of Christian missions to capture converts and for the resurgence of an unruly Moslem nationalism. They find themselves unable to serve as peacemakers between the Arab
states and Israel or to give a balanced picture. Today the missionary emphases
are underplayed; educational and philanthropic programs are substituted.

But their "concern" is not focused on the position of ethnic and religious
minorities in the Middle East, such as the Copts of Egypt, or the Assyrians
of Iraq, or the Armenians, or the Jews who reside in lands of Moslem faith.

What has been the condition of Jews in Moslem lands?

For thirteen centuries, the Jews in the Middle East lived on relatively friendly terms with their Arab neighbors; yet the record is marred by periodic persecutions.

In the seventh century, Mohammed expelled or exterminated Arab and Jewish tribes which refused to be converted to Islam. Later, the Moslems imposed a heavy poll tax on Jewish subjects.

In 807, the Caliph Harun-al-Rashid compelled all Jews to wear yellow badges. Later, local caliphs ordered Jews to wear black turbans.

In Moorish Spain during the so-called "Golden Age," Moslem measures of intolerance were imposed; the persecutions by Almohades in the twelfth century impelled the family of Moses Maimonides to leave Spain and wander across North Africa, finally to find haven in Cairo under the liberal rule of Saladin.

Discrimination against Jews in Arabic-speaking countries often reflected feudal ignorance and superstition. It lacked the specifically anti-Jewish animus which was characteristic of Christian Europe in later years. Despite periodic persecutions at times, Islam has a better record on the treatment of Jews than Christendom does.

At present, the status of Jews in the Arab lands varies. In Morocco, Algeria, and Tunisia, Jews are under the direct protection of the French government.

In Egypt, Jews have ostensibly the same rights as other nationals; but since the Arab-Israeli war, tension has increased alarmingly and the security of these Jews placed in jeopardy, so that many have left and have gone to Israel.

Jews are specifically banned from living in Saudi Arabia. In Yemen, Jews existed under cruelly repressive measures for centuries; only recently, the last remnants of the ancient Jewish communities were evacuated to Israel by air, in an epic operation called "The Magic Carpet."

In Lebanon, Jews are unmolested. During the 1948 war, many of the Maronite Christians guarded the Jewish community against attack from Moslem fanatics.

In Syria the condition of Jews has seriously deteriorated since Israel's establishment. The Iraqi government has consistently followed a policy of vindictiveness since its establishment after World War I. More than 100,000 Iraqi Jews chose to migrate to Israel, even though they were compelled to leave their property behind.

For Jews in Moslem lands, Israel is a haven of refuge from increasingly severe restrictions which have often degenerated into persecution.

CHAPTER EIGHT

The Specter of the Hammer and Sickle

How do Jews fare behind the Iron Curtain?

In the Soviet Union and the lands under its sway, there are about 2,500,-000 Jews — about 2,000,000 in the USSR, 250,000 in Rumania, 150,000 in Hungary, and less than 50,000 in Poland. They are denounced as "bourgeois" and "nationalists," accused of "cosmopolitanism" and of "deviations." Jewish enterprises have been confiscated or taken into "protective custody." Former owners of confiscated businesses and unemployed, propertyless artisans have been deported as "dangerous elements," and sent to slave-labor camps in Siberia or to remote areas of Hungary and Rumania.

For several years following Israel's recognition by the Soviet Union, emigration to Israel was permitted by the satellite countries but not by Russia itself. In 1951 the exit gates began to close.

Zionism had always been condemned by the Bolsheviks as "nationalist" and "imperialist," even before their seizure of power in 1917.

Anti-Jewish disturbances in Poland in 1946 and Hungary in 1946, 1947, and 1950 gave some indication of the pressure yet to come. The use of Hebrew and Yiddish was prohibited. Such philanthropic organizations as the American Joint Distribution Committee were falsely accused of serving in a network of Western espionage and their offices summarily closed. Many Jews were demoted from government positions and Jews disappeared from prominent posts in the press, arts, and sciences of Iron Curtain countries.

Although the Soviet Union later apparently seemed to soften its pressure against the Jews in Soviet countries, there was no indication that Soviet policy had been reversed. It had become clear to the world, however, that Israel was no ally of the Soviet Union in the battle between the free world and the Communist nations for control of the strategic Middle East.

What is Russia's attitude toward Zionism and the Jews?

Until the outbreak of overt anti-Semitism with the Rudolf Slansky trial in Prague in November 1952, the Communists insisted that within their orbit all races were treated equally. But their virulent attacks on the Jewish people and Israel made it clear that Jews were now subject to disabilities not shared in the same degree by other ethnic and cultural groups behind the Iron Curtain.

The motives seemed several: (1) an internal struggle for power among the Politburo leaders; (2) the traditional device of using Jews as a scapegoat to distract the masses from obvious domestic economic failure; (3) the strategy of capitalizing on anti-Jewish feeling among neo-Nazis of East Germany; and (4) an opportunistic move to win the anti-Israel forces of the Middle East.

Since Jews were predominantly middle class in status, the Communist onslaughts on the bourgeois system of property relations found the Jew a major target. The Marxist prejudice against organized religion directed an attack on Hebrew culture and on Judaic contributions to Western civilization; and Zionism felt the special virulence of the Soviet's hostility to Jewish nationalism.

In earlier years there had been anti-Semitic cartoons in Soviet newspapers; Jews purged from important posts would be identified by their adopted Russian name followed by the original Jewish name in parenthesis. But in the Prague trials the accused were officially designated as Jews and referred to as "Zionist spies." Even Jews who had offered to become assimilated found themselves liable for persecution as "dangerous elements."

This trend had been forecast by the swift liquidation of Jewish cultural institutions by the Soviet at the end of World War II. After forbidding Jewish schools to reopen, the Soviet closed down the only Jewish publishing house, Emes; and in 1948 the only Yiddish publication, *Einikeit,* disappeared mysteriously and suddenly. Prominent Yiddish writers and poets vanished without a trace.

Thus today, with a Jewish community of some 2,500,000 in the Soviet orbit, there is not a single Jewish school, Jewish publishing house, or Jewish newspaper. This Soviet anti-Semitism, if continued, presages a complete destruction of Jewish culture in the USSR.

51

VIEW OF HAIFA BAY

ROM MOUNT CARMEL

What effect has Israel had on the Soviet position in the Middle East?

The Soviet's vote for partition of Palestine in the face of its record of anti-Zionism has been interpreted as part of a strategy designed to divide the Middle East. Russia wanted Britain out of Palestine, in the hope of subsequently advancing her own interests in the region. Soviet leaders also apparently gambled on successfully exploiting both the Jewish working class and the small but noisy Jewish Communist Party in Palestine.

The Russians calculated inaccurately. Not only did the Jewish Communist Party fail to expand, never numbering more than 1,500 members; but the extreme left-wing segment of Israel's working class, the "Mapam" party, also failed to grow.

Israel, in short, rejected Communism. In the development of its democratic institutions, in its elections (where the maximum Communist vote was only 4 per cent — mostly from Arabs), and in its voting record at the United Nations, Israel unmistakably chose the way of the democracies.

Failing to gain a foothold in Israel, the Soviet Union reverted to its earlier hostility. Today Zionism is once again called a "tool of Western imperialism"; Jews are described as "cosmopolites" and "spies of the West." In such fashion the Kremlin may hope to intimidate Israel into tempering its friendship for the West. Russia has already created concern among Israelis over the fate of some 2,500,000 Jews locked behind the Iron Curtain.

The Soviet now apparently seeks to woo the Arab states by supporting their economic and propaganda war against Israel and by attempting to persuade them that Russia, not the United States, is their real friend. She wants to prevent the United States and the West from uniting the area and strengthening its psychological and physical resistance to Communism. It would be a serious blow to the USSR if the Arabs were to abandon their anti-Israel campaign and agree to make peace. For this would substantially advance what the Soviet Union fears most — a Middle East defense organization encompassing all the states of the region.

Israel is an effective barrier to Communist penetration of the Near and Middle East, a fact recognized with bitterness by the USSR. The hope of the world lies in encouraging the peoples of the Middle East to unite in the defense of freedom. Israel's own resistance to Communism can serve to strengthen the confidence of its neighbors in their own capacity to protect their independence and to prevent the growth of Communism in the Mediterranean area.

Is Communism making headway in the Mediterranean area?

One of the most important deterrents to the spread of Communism in the Middle East is the influence of Islam, now on the ascendant again in the wake of Arab nationalism. Islam opposes Communism because of Marxist materialism and because freedom of religion is denied to Moslems under Soviet rule. These two factors have helped to immunize the followers of Mohammed against the Communist virus.

Another important factor has been Communist tactical mistakes and failures. In accord with the theories of Marx and Lenin, the Communists have concentrated on the urban and industrial proletariat. But the Middle East is still predominantly agrarian — Iraq, 78 per cent; Jordan, 75 per cent; Syria and Lebanon, 70 per cent; Egypt, 68 per cent — with its population both peasant and serf. Communists failed to understand that Moslem land laws and customs, deeply rooted in Arab consciousness and regarded as integral to the faith of Islam, tended to prevent changes in land ownership. Such religious commands, coupled with Moslem fatalism, explained the political indifference so characteristic of the Arab *fellah*.

The Soviet Union has a new tactic — that of sending espionage agents, disguised as "pilgrims," to the holy city of Mecca. The purpose of these pseudo-Moslems? To convince the myriads of the devout assembled at the sacred Ka'bah that an "adapted" or "modified" communism would be a boon to the proletariat of Islam.

Communist ideology has had little success in any Arabic-speaking countries except perhaps Lebanon, where it has influenced a thin stratum of young intellectuals. But they have not provided leadership either for the urban proletariat or the *fellahin* because, for the most part, they are of upper class origin, remote socially and intellectually from the Arab masses.

The Communists' leadership has been handicapped by the national composition of the Middle East peoples. Minority groups like the Kurds, Armenians, Greeks, and others, have usually founded and controlled the Communist parties; but the national sensitivity of the region has prevented these men from emerging as real leaders to rally the masses. The number of recruits to the Communist Party has been remarkably low; and the ranks are not swelled by many fellow travelers or sympathizers. Israel has had the smallest enrollment (1,500) of any Communist Party, legal or illegal, in the entire area; and Lebanon the largest (about 12,000).

Communism can grow in the Middle East by the continuation of two factors: (1) a callous social policy on the part of Arab rulers; and (2) the Arab states' neutralist position on world issues.

CHAPTER NINE

Israel in the Family of Nations

How has Israel voted in the United Nations?

In the United Nations, Israel's stand has been, in virtually every instance, in accord with that taken by Western nations.

Israel joined in condemning the Korean aggression and in imposing an embargo on shipments of arms and strategic materials to North Korea and Communist China. Because of its own defense problems, Israel could not send troops to Korea, but it contributed medical supplies and processed food for civilian relief.

At the U.N. General Assembly in 1950, Israel voted for the establishment of a U.N. commission for the unification and rehabilitation of Korea and for elections to be held under U.N. auspices. In 1950, Israel supported the United States resolution which called upon member states to give full assistance to the Panmunjon negotiations and opposed the transfer of armistice proceedings to the General Assembly. In 1952, Israel vigorously upheld voluntary repatriation of prisoners of war. Unfortunately, the Arab states have no such record of consistent support of measures safeguarding the free world from aggression, for their stand has more often than not been "neutralist."

The Israel delegation voted against the Soviet resolution in 1950 which demanded withdrawal of all U.N. troops, except Republic of Korea soldiers; elections under Korean auspices with representation from both North and South; dispersal of the "illegal" U.N. Commission for Korea; and condemnation of "barbarous bombings" by the United States.

On disarmament and atomic energy, Israel voted with the Western nations to establish the disarmament commission and to provide for the reduction and control of all armaments and armed forces. Subsequently Israel voted against Soviet proposals to condemn the North Atlantic Treaty Organization and the United States Mutual Security Act.

Why does Israel oppose the internationalization of Jerusalem?

Jerusalem consists of two cities. The first is the Old City, now under Jordan control, a centuries-old walled enclosure about one mile square which contains most of the Holy Places. The second is the New City, or modern Jerusalem, whose history began with contemporary Zionist development in Palestine.

Both Jordanians and Israelis agree that the region to be internationalized is not a viable unit, geographically, economically, socially or politically.

Israel favors a *functional internationalization* of Jerusalem. This plan, supported by hundreds of distinguished Christian churchmen, empowers the U.N. to appoint an international commission to insure the safety and accessibility of the Holy Places, including those few in modern Jerusalem. The 160,000 inhabitants of the New City would not be subjected to foreign rule or suffer abridgment of civil and political rights.

When internationalization was first recommended in 1947, the Arabs summarily rejected both partition and internationalization. The Jewish representatives before the U.N. agreed to internationalization "with great reluctance and a heavy heart," and only in hope that their acceptance would hasten a peaceful settlement. Instead, Israel was invaded.

Faced first by Arab refusal and then by Arab shelling of Jerusalem, the U.N. was powerless. In the end, it was the army of Israel which saved the city and its inhabitants from annihilation.

New Jerusalem, surrounded on three sides by Arabs and linked to Israel by only a narrow corridor, cannot rely on the U.N. for protection. The New City is now completely integrated into the political, economic, administrative, and security structure of Israel.

Israel has followed a policy of scrupulous respect for the Holy Places in its area, and of careful attention to all other matters of concern to the international religious community. To this policy the Roman Catholic prelates in the region have given abundant witness, despite the Vatican's insistence on internationalization of *all* Jerusalem, old and new alike. The Vatican overlooks a significant precedent. When the Vatican City was established, there was no thought of including the entire city of Rome, although Rome had been under papal jurisdiction for centuries. The special status granted the Vatican City applied only to the Vatican buildings, St. Peter's, and some of the adjacent sites — not all the sacred spots in and around Rome. The parallel in the case of Jerusalem is clear.

Does Israel have expansionist ambitions?

Is Israel territorially aggressive, as many Arab leaders state?

Israel was the first to respond to the cease-fire orders of the U.N. Mediator during the 1948 war. Its government has consistently favored the transformation of the armistice agreements into peace treaties, with guarantees respecting territorial integrity.

In the light of their alarm over Israel's "expansion," the Arab states should be eager to conclude non-aggression pacts. But they refuse even to meet with Israel at the conference table.

Israel's high immigration rate was cited by the Arabs as proof that the young state would require additional territory. Today, Israel's opponents contend that the present boundaries are insufficient for additional immigrants, especially if the Iron Curtain were lifted and Jews poured in from the Soviet lands.

Israel has long since disproved the concept of limited "absorptive capacity" which the British had used as a rationale for curbing Jewish immigration. Its present boundaries enclose enough land to absorb many more immigrants. About half of the nation's population live in the three urban centers of Jerusalem, Tel Aviv-Jaffa, and Haifa. The country as a whole is sparsely settled. The Negev, comprising more than half of Israel's area, will be able to take at least two million additional immigrants when current irrigation and electrification programs are completed. Perhaps it should be noted that immigration into Israel dropped to 23,700 in 1952; and in 1953 there were indications of a desire on the part of some newcomers to emigrate *from* Israel.

Israel has neither the desire nor the capacity to venture beyond its borders for territorial gain. It must invest energies in making the desert yield rich crops and minerals which await only the application of modern science and hard work.

Even if one were to discount the peaceful assurances of such Israeli leaders as Prime Minister David Ben-Gurion and Foreign Minister Moshe Sharett, the problems still confronting the Israelis in their struggle to develop their land should make it clear that territorial ambitions and military forays would be both reckless and futile. The opposite is actually the case, for one Arab leader after another has declared, as did President Mohammed Naguib of Egypt, that the Israel "cancer" must be cut from the Arab world. An Iraqi statesman stated: "We will never make peace with the Jews." This, unfortunately, is the attitude that prevails in the Arab world.

CHRISTMAS MASS IN THE CATHEDRAL OF RATISBONNE IN THE NEW CITY OF JERUSALEM

Does Israel's existence endanger the West's oil resources in the Middle East?

On the contrary — the existence of Israel is one of the guarantees that the Western world will have a base from which these oil resources might be guarded.

Throughout the Palestine debate in the last ten years, those who tried to thwart the creation of the state of Israel and oppose American friendship toward Israel warned constantly that if a Jewish state were to be established, the Arab governments would deny their precious oil to the Western world.

Nothing of the sort has taken place.

In fact, in the five years since Israel's establishment, the U.S. companies interested in Middle Eastern oil have increased their stakes in the area, and the Arab countries have received increasing sums in oil royalties.

In 1948, the total amount paid to all Middle Eastern countries, including Iran, was $97 million.

In 1952, direct payments by oil companies to the Middle Eastern governments totaled $440 million — *excluding* Iran.

It should be emphasized that the loss of Iranian oil was in no way related to the establishment of Israel, for Iran and Israel are friendly nations and have diplomatic relations with each other. The Iranian oil flow to the West stopped because of Iran's struggle with Britain over the question of nationalization of oil refineries. The recent change in Iran's political fortunes indicates that the flow of oil from the abundant Iranian reserves may soon be resumed on an even greater scale than before. Israel's existence neither starts nor stops the process.

The threat to American oil holdings in the Middle East does not grow out of any danger that the Middle Eastern governments will voluntarily deprive themselves of this tremendous source of revenue, particularly after Iran's unhappy example. The real threat arises from the menace of Soviet penetration and aggression in this part of the world.

If the USSR were to invade the Middle East, it is doubtful whether any effective resistance could be put up by any of the countries there with the exception of Turkey and Israel, for most of the countries of the Middle East are not only immobilized by neutralism but can give only a token military account of themselves. The record of the Arab armies in the Arab-Israeli War of 1948 attests to that fact.

Only Turkey and Israel are ready and able to stand with the West in defense of the region against aggression. Without effective resistance, these oil resources would be lost to the United States.

What of Israel's future?

History has not decreed separate destinies for Israel and the other states of the Middle East, for Israel is at the center, a land bridge to its neighbors on the north, south, and east, a cultural bridge between the Arabic-speaking world and the West. As a geopolitical and economic unit, the region would have less coherence and cohesion if Israel were eliminated, or made only an enclave in a hostile environment.

When peace is established with the Arab neighbors and a sound economy achieved, Israel can become an industrial center for the predominantly agricultural Middle East and a processing chamber for commodities from the entire world. It will be a repository for technical skills and scientific knowledge, a conveyor of Western ideas, ideals, and techniques. With its venturesome spirit in the fields of soil development, irrigation, labor relations, and intercultural education, Israel will be a laboratory for other peoples in near-by lands, a pilot plant of the free world.

Israel can show the way for less advanced countries to a fuller life for all their citizens. Israel's proclamation of statehood, its defense against aggression from without, its development of democratic institutions, its rescue of homeless Jewry — all these are a testament to the power of spirit over matter, of dedication over resignation, of progress over retrogression.

All the nations of the Middle East region can work together, share their ideas and skills, and, in co-operative endeavor, improve their common lot. But friendship between Israel and the Arab lands is a basic essential, for the great Semitic peoples cannot fulfill their aspirations in a Mediterranean world half at war and half at peace.

Peace in the Middle East, a prerequisite for peace in the world, is the key to the future of the Arab states and of Israel. Only then can Israelis and Arabs, with the aid of the United Nations, effectively wage a common battle against the ills of that wide region: poverty, disease, illiteracy, religious conflicts, primitive theocracies, the exploitation of man by man.

Here lie great challenges. Israel, accepting those challenges, has already shown, and will continue to show, how life can become richer and fuller for the tens of millions who now live miserably in a vast feudal area and are desperately in need of man's ingenuity, man's devotion, and man's goodwill to make that part of the world truly blessed as in long times past.

Suggested Reading List

For the Near East as a whole:

Challenge and Response in the Middle East, by Hedley V. Cooke. Harper & Brothers.

Middle East Dilemmas, by J. C. Hurewitz. Harper & Brothers.

The United States and the Near East, by E. A. Speiser. Harvard University Press.

For Palestine:

Behind the Silken Curtain, by Bartley C. Crum. Simon & Schuster.

Palestine: A Study of Jewish, Arab and British Policies, by a group of distinguished scholars on behalf of the ESCO Foundation. Yale University Press.

History of Palestine: 139 A.D. to Modern Times, by James Parkes. Oxford University Press.

For the emergence of Israel:

New Star in the Near East, by Kenneth Bilby. Doubleday & Company.

The New State of Israel, by Gerald de Gaury. Frederick A. Praeger.

My Mission in Israel, by James G. McDonald. Simon & Schuster.

For Zionism:

Fulfillment: The Epic Story of Zionism, by Rufus Learsi. World Publishing Company.

Trial and Error: The Autobiography of Chaim Weizmann. Harper & Brothers.

For the Arab point of view:

The Arab Awakening, by George Antonius. J. B. Lippincott.

Palestine Is Our Business, by Millar Burrows. Westminster Press.

Palestine Dilemma, by Frank C. Sakran. Public Affairs Press.

For anti-Zionism:

A Partisan History of Judaism, by Elmer Berger. Devin-Adair Company.

If the reader desires a longer bibliography, he may obtain one by writing to the author in care of the publisher of this book.

Index

Date Due

NO 1 5'57	MAR 6 1984		
OCT 27 '61	MAY 1 0 '88		
DEC 16 '62			
MY 9 '63			
DE 30 '64			
MR 24 '66			
Apr. 11			
18'66			
AG 1 6 '67			
MAR 22 '68 APR 9 '68)			
JUN 9 '69			
I N			
JUL 1 4 '70			
J N			
SEP 26 '71			
OCT 10 '71			
MAR 6 '84